# EMAKI

# *Emaki*

## JAPANESE
## PICTURE
## SCROLLS

by Hideo Okudaira

Charles E. Tuttle Company
Rutland, Vermont & Tokyo, Japan

European Representatives:

Continent:

BOXERBOOKS, INC., Zurich

British Isles:

PRENTICE-HALL INTERNATIONAL, INC., London


Produced by Toto Shuppan Company, Limited

Tokyo, Japan

for the Charles E. Tuttle Company of

Rutland, Vermont and Tokyo, Japan with

editorial offices at

15 Edogawa-cho, Bunkyo-ku, Tokyo

Library of Congress Catalog

Card No. 62-20798


First edition, 1962


Cover design by Masakazu Kuwata

incorporating calligraphy by Ichimatsu Tanaka

Manufactured in Japan

# Foreword

THE term *emaki* refers to the type of picture scroll produced in large numbers in Japan in ancient and medieval times, i.e., from the tenth to the sixteenth century. Widely varied in subject matter, they illustrate, usually with accompanying text, literary works, moral tales, biographies, and legends concerning the origin of celebrated shrines and temples. The number of works extant today is approximately one hundred and twenty, comprising some six hundred scrolls in all. The names of close to one hundred other works now lost are known to us through old records; these account for nearly four hundred further scrolls, counting only those works where the number of scrolls is known. It is clear from this that Japan must have produced vast quantities of these *emaki*.

The seven centuries during which the form, which originated in China, was produced in Japan saw it popular among many different classes of society, from court nobles and warriors to the priesthood and the common people. It plays a peculiarly important role, thus, in the nation's cultural and artistic history. A further important characteristic of the *emaki* is that almost every work has its basis in literature or in some popular moral tale. The form, in fact, might be called an artistic projection of the joys and sorrows of humanity, and the continued popularity of such subject-matter over a long period—it can almost be considered a tradition—shows how the Japanese in ancient and medieval times looked to pictures to provide them with stories and a wide range of human emotion.

This strong story-telling element in the *emaki* presupposes also the predominance of human figures. In some works, a full one hundred, sometimes as many as two or three hundred, persons appear in one scroll, ranging over the whole of society from Emperor to peasant. For this reason, the scrolls are of incomparable value as sources of information on life and customs in bygone Japan. There is a similar diversity in the artists who produced the *emaki*. Professional artists included the painters in the service of the court and of shrines and temples, as well as unknown, humble artists in the capital and the provinces, and their ranks were swelled by many amateur enthusiasts, among them the Emperor, members of the Imperial family, court nobles, and high priests.

The *emaki* is painted in the *yamato-e* style. This style, peculiar to Japan, ranges from the richest coloring to simple lines in ink monochrome, and is admirably fitted to the portrayal of Japanese people, manners, and scenery in all their diversity. Throughout their development, the form and the style were inextricably bound up together, and for this reason a study of the *emaki* is of the greatest significance in the history of art also.

Subject matter and style apart, not the least astonishing feature of these works is the extraordinary skill with which they solve the problems of composition and organization presented by this unique art form, in which the viewer himself moves and changes the picture before him with his own hands. In this connection, the reader should bear in mind that the *emaki* is intended to be viewed from right to left—the opposite, that is, of the direction in which he is accustomed to looking at Western books.

I should like to express my thanks to Mr. John Bester, who translated the main text, and Mr. Charles Pomeroy, who translated the appendices.

May, 1962

Hideo Okudaira

# Contents

# List of Color Plates

# List of Plates

# Plate 1
# The Complete First Scroll from *Shigi-san Engi*

See page 170 for an explanation of *Shigi-san Engi*. As explained in the foreword, the scrolls are viewed from right to left. Arrows are inserted to indicate the direction. The first scroll of *Shigi-san Engi* contains no narrative text, but the story is known from a legend, popular at the time, which appears in the *Uji Shūi Monogatari*.

1   E *Ingakyō* (page 168)

2  *Genji Monogatari Emaki* (page 168)

3  *Shigi-san Engi* (page 170)

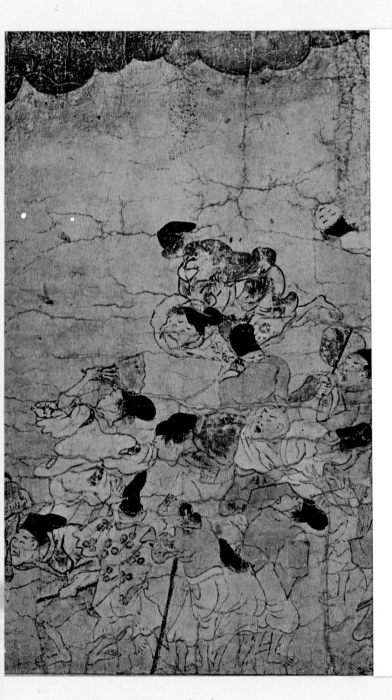

4   *Ban Dainagon Ekotoba* (page 171)

5   *Go-sannen Kassen Emaki* (page 68)

6   *Jigoku Zōshi* (page 175)

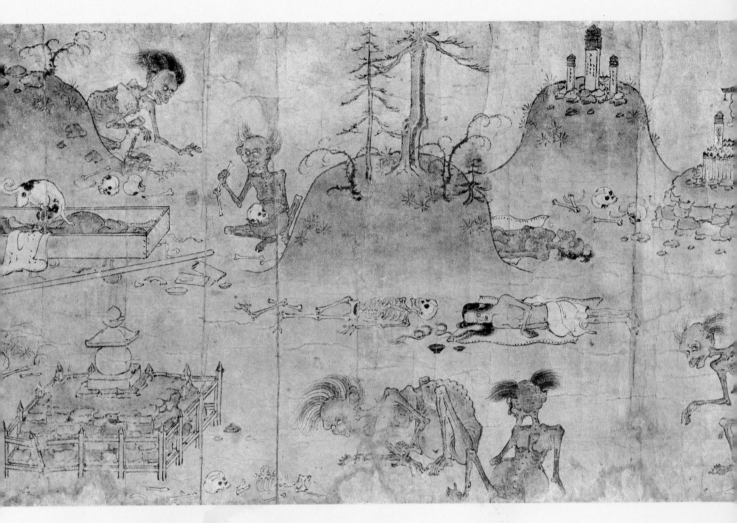

7  *Gaki Zōshi* (page 176)

8   *Kegon Engi* (page 179)

9 *Kitano Tenjin Engi* (page 183)

10   *Sanjūroku Kasen Emaki* (page 184)

11 *Heiji Monogatari Emaki* (page 186)

12 *Ippen Shōnin Eden* (page 192)

# History

JUST as Japanese culture as a whole first developed largely under the influence of Chinese culture, so what is known in Japan as the *emaki,* or picture scroll, was first suggested by similar scrolls from China.

It is not clear just when the Chinese first conceived the idea of painting pictures on a horizontal scroll. In China, however, the scroll is older than any other form of book, and it seems likely that the picture scroll was only a natural sequel to the original written scroll. While the paper picture scrolls of Egypt ran from left to right, the picture scrolls of China and Japan run, as does their ordinary writing, from right to left.

Though the date when picture scrolls were first produced is not clear, reference in the *Litai Minghua-chi,* a celebrated work on the theory and history of painting edited by Chan Yenyüan, shows that works in this form already existed under the Han dynasty in the first century A.D. The same source also shows that subsequently, throughout the Chin dynasty, the Six Dynasties and the Sui dynasty on into the T'ang dynasty (third to seventh century A.D.) there appeared a succession of first-rate artists, and that many of the rulers were art lovers who made collections of celebrated old works.

The T'ang dynasty saw a great flowering of Chinese culture. Painting flourished, and the number of picture scrolls produced was considerable. (A number of copies of scrolls of this period still survive today.) The taste for old-style painting continued to flourish in the subsequent Five Dynasties and Sung ages. Though it is rash to assume that every use of the word "scroll" in ancient Chinese catalogues and histories of art refers to a picture scroll—some of them may have been hanging scrolls like the Japanese *kakemono*—it would seem that, all in all, the output of such scrolls was considerable. Generally speaking, Chinese painting up to and including T'ang times would seem to have consisted principally of murals and horizontal scrolls, while from Sung times on, the hanging scroll took their place. The records mentioned above suggest that the total number of picture scrolls produced in China from Han to T'ang times was truly enormous.

In view of this continued popularity of the picture scroll in ancient China and the subsequent development of the form in Japan also, it is evident, if one also takes into account the history of cultural exchanges between Japan and the mainland, that a number of these Chinese scrolls must have been brought across to Japan. Nothing is known at present as to the date when this took place. Nevertheless, it seems likely that the scrolls were imported, together with other books and paintings, around the time when Buddhism was first introduced into Japan and the way was thus paved for a great influx of Buddhistic culture from the continent. For the purpose of this work, it is convenient to make the introduction of Buddhism into Japan the starting point of our history.

## The Asuka and Nara Periods (552-794)

As we have already seen, it is not clear at what point during this period Chinese picture scrolls were first imported into Japan, nor is anything known as to their nature and quality. Assuming, however, that a certain number were brought in by ship during the period, it would seem probable, in view of the nature and background of the culture of the age, that the majority of them had some connection with Buddhism.

Buddhism was introduced into Japan about the middle of the sixth century and, thanks to the efforts of Shōtoku Taishi in the reign of the Empress Suiko (early seventh century), soon became firmly rooted. With the Nara period (eighth century), it achieved a great popularity. During this period, sutras began to be imported from China—at first, via Korea, from the China of the Six Dynasties, then later, with the despatch of envoys to Sui and T'ang China, directly from China itself. With the increasing popularity of Buddhism, however, these imported scriptures became inadequate to meet the demand, so the only solution was to make more copies of them in Japan. The oldest record of the transcription of scriptures in Japan is an account in the *Nihon Shoki* of how the Buddhist Tripitaka was transcribed for the first time—at the Kawahara-dera Temple, in March, 673.

With the enormous increase in the popularity of Buddhism in the Nara period, transcription of the scriptures also reached its greatest height. Centers for this work were established by temples, by the aristocracy, and by private persons in the provinces, the largest of them all being the official bureau set up by the government. This bureau, which employed between two and three hundred workers—including scribes, proof readers, and binders—produced many copies of the original scriptures.

←　1　*E Inga-kyō*

臣並言汝女對今宜
堪此舉今欲相屈時
摩訶那摩荅王使言
謹奉勅音王即令諸
臣擇採吾曰遣車萬
巳其之太子婚姻之
乘而往近之凱至宮
礼又復更增諸伎女
衆盍夜娛樂尒時太
子恒興其妃行住坐
卧未曾不俱初自无
有世俗之意於靜夜
中但備禪觀時王曰
日問諸綵女太子興
妃相接近不綵女荅
言不見太子有夫婦
道王聞此語慈憂不
之如是經時稍不接
樂更憎伐女而娛樂
近時王深疑恐不能
男
介時太子聞諸伐女
歌詠園林華菓茂盛
流泉清涼太子忽便
欲出遊観即遣伐女
往白王言在宮日久
樂欲輙出園林遊戲
王聞此語心生歡喜
而自合言太子當是

It is among the surviving scriptures copied during this period that one finds the earliest extant specimen of the picture scroll—the *E Inga-kyō*. This work, an illustrated version of the *Sutra of Cause and Effect* (Color Pl. 1, Fig. 1) relates the life-story of the Buddha—his birth, his leaving home, his religious activities, and his final entry into Nirvana. There are several different translations of this sutra, this *E Inga-kyō* being based on the four-volume version translated by Kunabattara, who lived during the Chinese Southern Dynasty. The scroll is divided horizontally into two portions, the lower half containing the text of the sutra, the upper half illustrations corresponding to the text below. Though it is thus no more than a sutra scroll with illustrations, it nevertheless constitutes a form of *emaki*. Versions extant today are in the possession of the Jōbon-Rendai-ji Temple, the Hōon-in Temple, the Tokyo University of Arts, and the Masuda family (all of these in one scroll). Portions also survive in the Kuni and Yasuda families, though these are not cut from the same scroll.

The roller of the Hōon-in version bears an inscription "seventh day of the fourth month, scribe of the lower eighth rank." It is clear from this that the scroll was made by a scribe of the official bureau mentioned above, and since this practice of giving ranks to the scribes who copied sutras began in the Tempyō era under the Emperor Shōmu, the Hōon-in version would seem to be a product of this era.

The Chinese characters in the text of these extant versions are in the T'ang style of writing typical of scribes of the Tempyō era. The details of the pictures are all outlined crudely in India ink, which is filled in with vermilion, scarlet, crimson, green, yellow, white and other bright colors. Again, the style of the pavilions, the dress worn by the figures, and the way in which trees and stones are depicted all show an indebtedness to the painting of Six Dynasties China. Moreover, this kind of illustrated sutra scroll, in which pictures and text are aligned horizontally, is reportedly also to be found among the sutra scrolls unearthed at Tung-huan. Thus it is almost certain that illustrated scrolls of this kind were not a Japanese invention but copies of originals brought from China.

The question arises of whether, in addition to these religious works, the age produced any *emaki* designed primarily to give esthetic pleasure. As we have already seen, picture scrolls were produced in China from a very early period. At first, they were mostly religious and didactic in purpose but later they also came to depict historical events, antiquities, Taoist and Buddhist celebrities, contemporary customs and personages, landscapes, birds and beasts, and so on. It would seem not unlikely, therefore, that the Nara period also saw the import of this kind of picture. Among the Imperial relics in the Shōsō-in there are some pictures—the *Torige Tachi Onna* Screen (a portrait, decorated with feathers, of a standing woman), for instance—which depict non-religious subjects, while the Emperor

Shōmu is recorded as having possessed other similar screens, which have not survived. Since such large-scale examples of T'ang style painting were imported into Japan, it would be rash to assert that no specimens of non-didactic T'ang picture scrolls—a far smaller form—came into the country. One thing that is doubtful, however, is whether, even assuming the import of a considerable number of non-religious scrolls, the predominantly Buddhistic flavor of the culture of the Asuka and Nara Japan permitted them much influence on artistic circles in this country. It would, however, at the very least, have given an impetus to the understanding and appreciation of Chinese picture scrolls among the people of Japan.

In summary, the age saw the gradual import into Japan of the Chinese picture scroll and the creation in this country of a certain degree of interest in the form. It stands prior to the birth of the truly Japanese *emaki,* and the mere existence of the *E Inga-kyō* is not enough to justify this work as the ultimate source of the *emaki.* Before the purely Japanese *emaki* could appear, it was necessary for a truly native culture to develop at home to give it nourishment.

## The Heian Period (794 - 1185)

Though generally considered as one unit, the Heian period covers four centuries, from the removal of the capital to Heian (Kyoto) in 794 to the collapse of the Taira family in 1185. It is customary in histories of Japanese art to divide the period into two halves, with the halting of envoys to T'ang China in 894 as the turning point. In discussing the development of the Heian *emaki,* however, I have divided the period into three—Early Heian, from the removal to the new capital up to the halting of envoys to China (794-894), in which the influx into Japan of the Chinese picture scroll continued from the previous age; Middle Heian, up to the beginning of government by the cloistered emperors (894-1086), which saw the birth and development of the first purely Japanese *emaki;* and Late Heian, up to the collapse of the Tairas (1086-1185), which saw the Japanese *emaki* in its full glory.

## 1) Early Heian (794-894)

In this age, as in the preceding Nara period, society was dominated by T'ang culture. There was much traffic between Japan and T'ang China, and the import and imitation of Chinese culture continued as ever. The capital, Heian, was itself modeled on Ch'ang An, the capital of T'ang China, while a large number of official ceremonies, as well as the habits and amusements of the aristocracy, were based on T'ang models. In the fields of learning and literature likewise, great respect was paid to the Chinese classics and to the Chinese style of writing. The writing of Chinese poems was exceedingly popular, and the music most favored at court was T'ang music.

The same was true of painting. Along with the scriptures, the priests and scholars who visited T'ang China brought back with them a large number of religious paintings, which created a fad for painting similar works in Japan. Non-religious works also, on Chinese themes and using Chinese forms and techniques, were produced and admired by the aristocratic society of the time. In the Imperial palace and the mansions of the nobility the form of the murals to be found in the palaces of China was adapted to suit Japanese needs, and large-scale paintings in the T'ang style were painted on sliding doors and screens.

Thus this age was one in which Chinese literature and art were greatly prized. At the same time, in China itself, T'ang picture scrolls were being produced in great quantities. It can probably be assumed, therefore, that a number of these T'ang scrolls were imported and were admired among the Japanese aristocracy. There is a story which tells how, towards the end of the period in question, the Prince Tsunesada (died 886), son of the Emperor Junna, was presented with a scroll entitled *Ensoku-zu* but declared it was a shameful thing and burnt it. Whether this scroll was imported from China or made in Japan is not clear, but it shows at least that pictures in the form of illustrated scrolls were already popular in this period. Again, a work written about 891 by Fujiwara Sase, in which, at the command of the Emperor Uda, he compiled a list of all Chinese works existing in Japan at the time, contains many titles including the word "illustrated." These are all pre-T'ang works, so most of them were probably scrolls. They were, of course, only books with illustrations that cannot be called true picture scrolls. Even so, they doubtlessly served to show the Japanese the possibilities of allying pictures and text, and it only remained to give the pictures an importance equal to or greater than that of the text for something close to the *emaki* to emerge.

## 2)  Middle  Heian (894 - 1086)

This was the period during which the Fujiwara regency was most powerful, and during which aristocratic culture centering around the Fujiwara family bloomed in all its glory.   While the early Heian period had devoted itself almost entirely to the imitation of T'ang culture, towards its end— about the time, that is, when Japan stopped sending envoys to T'ang China—there appeared the first signs of a more native culture.   There had been, for instance, the "six poetical sages" famous for their *waka,* and the *Taketori Monogatari,* the first romance in Japanese literature.   Some screen paintings, too, which appeared in the 870's under the Emperor Seiwa, had depicted such Japanese scenes as autumn leaves floating down the Tatsuta River.

With the subsequent cessation of envoys to T'ang China, a purely Japanese taste in art and literature came more and more to the fore. Traffic between China and Japan was not of course wholly severed, and trade between the two countries went on even after the missions stopped, but T'ang culture was nevertheless already losing its control over Japan. After the cessation of envoys and the collapse in 907 of the T'ang dynasty, this T'ang culture was to be replaced to a remarkable degree by the newly emerging native culture.   The next 200 years were to see the sudden flowering of the art and literature of the tenth and eleventh centuries, the two peak periods being the Engi and Tenryaku eras and the age, centering around Michinaga, when the power of the Fujiwaras was at its zenith.

In the fifth year of Engi (905) the *Kokinshū,* the first Imperial anthology of *waka*, was compiled.   This historic venture heralded the compilation of a series of Imperial anthologies of native *waka,* in contrast to the early Heian period, when Imperial anthologies of Chinese poetry had been greatly in vogue.   At the same time, the coming into widespread use of the *kana* syllabary paved the way for a truly Japanese literature and eventually brought about the great age of "*kana* literature" and of the romances.   Screen painting also came into sudden vogue, as is shown by the extraordinary number of *waka* in the *Kokinshū* and other anthologies of this age which were inspired by screen or *shōji* paintings.   These paintings dealt chiefly with Japanese beauty spots, customs, yearly observances and the like.   The use of things Japanese as a subject for such paintings increased suddenly from the beginning of the tenth century.

Under the influence of this sudden emergence of a native Japanese culture and art, the picture-scroll, similarly, was to make a new start as the truly Japanese *emaki*.   No *emaki* of this period are extant today, and one must rely for any knowledge of them on contemporary accounts in the romances and anthologies.   The accounts given by the *Genji Monogatari* are particularly informative on this score, showing just how enthusiastically *emaki* were produced and admired among the aristocracy of the day.   The setting of *Genji* is obviously the middle of the tenth century—about half a century, that is, before the age of the authoress, Murasaki Shikibu.   The "E-awase" chapter, moreover, relates that in the Engi and Tenryaku eras (the first half of the tenth century), *emaki* were extremely popular among the court nobles.   Again, it seems probable that the reason why Murasaki Shikibu drew on *emaki* to such an important extent for her subject matter was that at the time of writing, the age of the Emperor

Ichijō (986-1011), when Michinaga was at the height of his power, there existed a great number of *emaki* and that she had seen them herself. The *Genji Monogatari* (Tales of Genji), of course, is only a piece of fiction, but the social manners and conditions it portrays can be taken as reflecting to a certain degree the realities of the age.

One thing that is clear from *Genji Monogatari,* particularly the "E-awase" chapter, is that at the time of the Emperor Reizei a considerable number of *emaki* were surviving from earlier times, and that new *emaki* were being produced constantly. It is also clear that they were very varied in content, ranging from illustrations of the "diaries" popular in literature at the time to pictures of the seasons and annual observances, as well as illustrations of old romances such as the *Taketori Monogatari, Ise Monogatari,* and *Utsubo Monogatari* and contemporary narratives based on out-of-the-way happenings. Others, again, apparently drew on old Chinese stories. It is also clear that scrolls such as the *Utsubo Monogatari Emaki,* where the story was set in both Japan and China, were painted in a mixture of the T'ang and *yamato-e* styles of painting, while both the *sumi-e* and *tsukuri-e* techniques (to be described later) were in use at the time. In particular, the new works of the age of the Emperor Reizei were, the *Genji Monogatari* relates, of unsurpassed beauty and technical brilliance. These beautiful paintings were accompanied by texts written by celebrated calligraphists of the day, while the paper used, the rollers, and the covers were all of the finest materials available.

Thus from accounts such as these we learn that the picture scroll around the Engi and Tenryaku eras was aristocratic, esthetic, and decorative in the extreme; in content, it was predominantly literary and secular. Why, one may ask, should this particular age have seen the appearance of a truly Japanese picture scroll—Japanese both in spirit and subject matter?

As we have seen, the Nara period and early Heian period had already brought the Japanese into contact with Chinese picture scrolls, or with illustrated books in scroll form. The stimulus that, after such a long period of passive appreciation, led to the creation of a Japanese picture scroll was the already mentioned upsurge of a native culture. The influence on the *emaki* of this new trend, and in particular of the sudden vogue for the courtly romance in literature, must have been considerable. At the time, screens and sliding doors which bore pictures often had pasted on them strips of paper bearing verses celebrating those pictures. *Ashide-e* also appeared, which used the letters of verses written in cursive *kana* script to form pictures of rushes, water, etc. People were already accustomed, thus, to the union of visual art and literature; the purely esthetic picture at the time fell, in fact, within the province of literature. This made it only natural, when the courtly romance came suddenly into fashion, that it should join forces with the newly emerging *emaki*. Frequent references to *e-monogatari* (picture-stories) and *monogatari-e* (story-pictures) are to be found scattered throughout such works as the *Yamato Monogatari,* the *Genji Monogatari* and, a little later, the *Eiga Monogatari*. This marriage of story and picture in the scroll form was to continue for long years as one of the principal characteristics of the Japanese *emaki*.

There are various reasons why the newly-born Japanese *emaki* should have achieved such immediate popularity in this age. One is that, unlike the Buddhist paintings and paintings on screens and sliding doors, which by their nature call for an expert artist, the picture scroll can be done by the amateur painter. This made it a particularly popular pastime among the aristocrats of the time, who included many talented amateur artists. Another reason is that the picture scroll, being small and easy to handle, afforded an amusement ideally suited to the indoor, pleasure-loving life of the aristocrats. It fitted in admirably with the current taste for the miniature: as the authoress of *Makura no Sōshi* says, "anything small is particularly attractive." The scroll, moreover, though small in size, would unroll to reveal an unexpected length of picture and a considerable diversity of scene. One need only unroll it gently on the table before one to be presented with a momentarily changing succession of scenes, portraying life in all its different aspects. It is easy to imagine how this must have appealed to the aristocrats of the time, who usually spent all day indoors with nothing to do but amuse themselves.

Yet another factor which contributed to the popularity of the *emaki* was the already-mentioned vogue for picture contests. The art of the picture scroll, besides being the ideal pastime, was also the ideal social sport for the aristocrats of the day. In order to emerge victor in such contests, one must find increasingly interesting subjects, more skilful ways of presenting them, more beautiful paper and backings, and one must strive to startle others with one's originality. To avoid monotony in the subject matter, tales rich in incident were eagerly sought after, and a decorative, artificial kind of beauty came into vogue. It can be seen, thus, how the picture scroll that came into being at this time was encouraged to develop literary and decorative characteristics by the favor it found among the aristocracy.

What has preceded refers to the scroll designed to give esthetic pleasure. Of religious scrolls of this period there are, similarly, no extant examples. However, while there is detailed information available concerning the secular scroll, there is almost none concerning its religious counterpart. The one thing we have is a record that in 984, under the Emperor Kazan, Minamoto no Tamenori had a work in three scrolls called the *Sambō Ekotoba* made for Princess Sonshi. The original work does not survive, but a copy of the text still extant shows that the first scroll dealt with the story of the Buddha's birth, the second with biographies of and miraculous tales about celebrated Japanese priests, and the third with annual rituals celebrated at various temples. Opinion has always been divided as to whether the work was an *emaki* or not. If it was, and text and pictures alternated in each chapter, then the work may well have been a full-blown specimen of the religious *emaki*. However, at the moment nothing points to any great development of the religious *emaki* in this period. The failure of the genre to develop, after the fine start made by the *E Inga-kyō* in the Nara period, may possibly be due to the overwhelming popularity of the paintings of esoteric Buddhism at the time. Or possibly the decorated versions of the sutras which, according to the *Eiga Monogatari,* the ladies-in-waiting of the Empress Dowager were making with such exquisite care in the year 1021 were enough to satisfy their urge to create religious works. It should be noted that these "decorated sutras" (e.g., the *Heike Nōkyō*) differ from the *E Inga-kyō* in that they included pictures merely as decoration around the text, and not as an integral part of the scroll.

To sum up the development of the picture scroll from the tenth into the eleventh century, the period from the reigns of the Emperors Daigo and Murakami to that of the Emperor Ichijō (897-1036) saw the emergence of the truly Japanese *emaki* from among the court nobles and aristocracy. The same period saw the non-religious *emaki,* with its love of stories and its decorative, largely aristocratic qualities, being produced and appreciated on a large scale. In this sense, the age saw both the birth and the efflorescence of the purely Japanese *emaki.*

## 3) Late Heian (1086 - 1185)

The aristocratic culture of the Heian period, which had developed parallel with the power of the Fujiwara family, reached its peak in the time of Michinaga. Then—again like the Fujiwaras—it found itself at a halt. Subject to no stimulus from abroad, isolated within the narrow confines of the Imperial capital, it produced all it was to produce within one short period, then lost its power of originality and began steadily to stagnate.

The collapse of the ancient society centering around the court and the birth of a medieval feudal society are generally regarded as having taken place during the period from the tenth on into the eleventh and twelfth centuries. The system of government by "cloistered Emperors" which took the place of the Fujiwara regency was, indeed, a decadent and abnormal phenomenon, and it soon collapsed. During the constant squabbling among the nobles that followed, the warrior class slowly but surely increased its power. The court aristocracy, its old security and assurance gone, lost more and more of its former brilliance. As a result, the culture of the age of "cloistered Emperors," far from being a development of that of the Fujiwara regency, was basically incapable of producing anything new at all.

Out of the stagnation of the age there emerged a tendency to worship the past, a nostalgia for the days of the Fujiwara regency. One result of this tendency was a vogue for historical literature which attempted to recapture the glories of the past—the *Eiga Monogatari,* for instance— and for imitations of earlier works such as the *Genji Monogatari.* Another was the increasing respect for tradition in learning and the arts, along with a fashion for the esoteric transmission and for antiquities.

Yet another result, of quite a different nature, was the spread to the aristocracy of elements from the culture of the common people, a culture that was at a lower level than and of different stock from their own. Encouraged by the stagnation of the old aristocratic culture and by the search of the nobility itself for something new, popular songs and dances—*sarugaku, dengaku, imayō, riyō,* and their like—came into favor. In literature, too, there appeared a new type of work—e.g., the *Konjaku Monogatari*—which dealt with characters such as warriors and people from the provinces, who hitherto had scarcely been recognized as human beings, and which used for its themes the stories of martial prowess and the comic or vulgar tales popular among the lower classes. The aristocratic culture of this age (twelfth century) had, thus, already lost the absolute quality it possessed in the preceding tenth and eleventh centuries.

The civil wars of Hogen and Heiji (1156-1159), which sprang from the breakdown of the "cloistered Emperor" system and internal dissension among the court nobility, resulted in the accession to power of the Taira family. The Tairas, however, failed to produce anything new in the cultural field. Instead, they concentrated on imitations of the Fujiwara culture, and in this sense their age can perhaps be considered as an extension of the age of the cloistered Emperors, as the final burst of glory of the aristocratic culture of the Heian period.

The same combination of worship of the past and interest in the new realities of the present that we have already seen above was reflected in the picture scroll, to which it lent, unexpectedly, a new diversity and brilliance. It is among the products of this twelfth century that one finds the greatest masterpieces ever achieved in this genre—works such as the *Genji Monogatari Emaki* (Tales of Genji), the *Shigi-san Engi* (Legends of Shigi-san Temple), the *Ban Dainagon Ekotoba* (Story of the Courtier Ban Dainagon), and the *Chōjū Giga* (Cartoons of Animals). Of the *Genji Monogatari Emaki* (Fig. 2, Color Pl. 2), based on the now world-famous classic of the Heian period, there remain today only four scrolls, and these have been cut up, separating the pictures and the text, in order to make preservation easier. These scrolls contain 19 pictures and 20 sections of the text. It seems likely, however, that the scrolls originally covered the 54 chapters of the novel in their entirety, so that even if a minimum of two or three scenes from each chapter were illustrated, the work must have been of a considerable scale.

The text of the scroll is written in graceful, flowing *kana* script on the finest paper which is inlaid with gold flakes, gold dust, fine silver

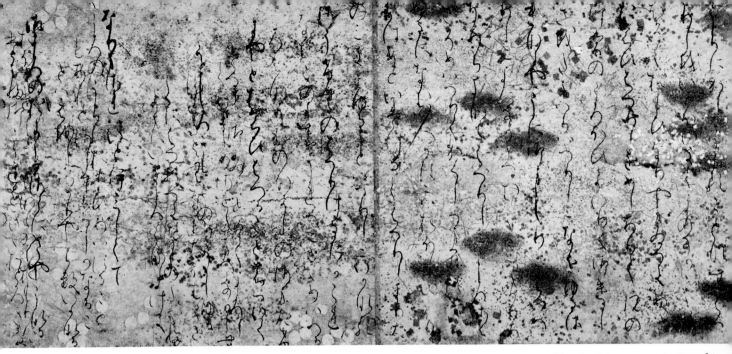

stripes, and floral patterns. Each portion of the text is followed by a picture, each picture, in the manner of an illustration, portraying only one scene from the many events related. Most of the scenes shown are the interiors of mansions of the nobility, and a characteristic "bird's-eye view" technique is adopted whereby the roofs are removed to allow the rooms and their occupants to be viewed from above. Another characteristic technique is employed for the faces of the ladies and gentlemen of the aristocracy. The eyes are represented by two single curved lines, the nose by a single hook (Figs. 3 & 76); the effect created is placid and expressionless, reminding one of the face of a sleeper. The result is that all the characters are prototypes, devoid of any individuality of their own.

The painting technique used is that known as *tsukuri-e*. Each object in the picture is first outlined with a fine black line, then everything is filled in with heavy colors which cover every inch of the space available. The total effect, with the refined, rich colors so tastefully combined, is close to that of the purely decorative picture. The way in which every inch of the background is heavily painted in, imprisoning spatially the human beings portrayed before it, combines with the placid, almost com-

3   *Genji   Monogatari   Emaki*   (Detail)

*Genji Monogatari Emaki* (Detail)

63

atose expression of the faces to emphasize still further the prevailing calm. All strong effects of light and shade are eschewed; everything is gentle, lyrical.

Nowhere, perhaps, more clearly than in this *Genji Monogatari* scroll can one read the longing of the aristocracy of this age for the departed glories of Fujiwara society. The beautiful designs that embellish the paper, the graceful letters written on it, the elegant forms of the nobles and their ladies, painted in such sumptuous colors—all represent the ultimate in delicate, painstaking technique, the highest peak of the romantic *emaki*.

The Genji scrolls have long been attributed to Fujiwara Takayoshi, but from the style and technique it is clear that they are the work of several hands and not one single artist. This is true of the text as well as the pictures. It would seem, however, that the work was produced under the direction of one mastermind who conceived the plan for the whole and was responsible for selecting the materials and the artists. Such an elaborate production could only have been undertaken in response to an order from some very exalted quarter, and the work probably represents a desperate attempt by the aristocracy of the time to recreate the culture of the Fujiwara age. The *tsukuri-e* style and the arrangement of the

scroll in short, alternating sections of text and picture almost certainly originated at an early date and were followed faithfully, with further refinements of technique, in the *Genji* scroll. It can, in fact, be looked on as a conservative work carrying on with the utmost faithfulness the traditions of a previous age.

The *Shigi-san Engi* and the *Ban Dainagon Ekotoba,* on the other hand, are products of the new age. For its subject matter, the former (Fig. 4, Color Pl. 3) abandons the typical courtly classic typified by *Genji* and uses a narrative, something in the nature of a popular legend, which is also recorded in the *Konjaku Monogatari*. It combines two stories— the story of a miracle that happens to a devout priest at the Shigi-san monastery in Yamato Province, and the story of his discovery by his sister, a nun, who has not seen him since he left home 20 years before. Though it is in one sense the biography of a man of religion, the emphasis is less on piety than on popular, narrative interest. Again, though there is one incident relating to court life, the prevailing tone of the whole is plebeian. What is more, the artist does not see his common people merely as figures serving to illustrate social manners and customs, but approaches them with a more positive curiosity, as representatives of the new order that is just evolving. There is much in common here with the new interest shown by the author of *Konjaku Monogatari* in what one might call the "untamed beauty" of these lower classes of society.

In its style just as in its subject matter, the *Shigi-san Engi* contrasts strongly with the *Genji* scrolls. Throughout all three scrolls of the *Shigi-san Engi,* there are only four pieces of text, the story being unfolded in one long, almost unbroken painting which shows each development in chronological sequence. The effect is one of flow and vitality, so that the viewer is drawn on irresistibly by the unfolding of the narrative. The dynamic movement contrasts strongly with the mood of inscrutability in which the *Genji* scrolls are steeped.

In place of the *tsukuri-e* style used in *Genji,* we find a new style that places emphasis on line, a style at once light, rhythmical, and admirably suited to the expression of movement and speed. Since the subjects dealt with are largely plebeian, the "bird's-eye view" of interiors is abandoned in favor of outdoor settings. The movements of the characters, similarly, are lively, and the portrayal of the faces emphasizes particular characteristics to the extent that it verges on caricature. Here again, the style is utterly different from that of the *Genji* scrolls, where the faces are devoid of all individuality.

Where the *Genji* scroll is quietistic and romantic, the *Shigi-san Engi* is dynamic, realistic, dramatic. Where the former is lyrical, the latter is narrative and descriptive. Such dynamic, realistic, descriptive elements had hitherto been unknown in the *emaki,* and in this sense the *Shigi-san Engi* clearly marks the beginning of the new age. A further point specially worthy of note is the way the picture in the *Shigi-san* scroll is no longer cut up into short sections, but united in one constantly flowing, unbroken scene in which the story is carried skilfully forward in terms of form and space. (See Plate 1)

The result is epoch-making in the history of painting in that, by clever use of a unique form—the picture scroll—the possibility of chronological development has for the first time been given to a medium normally only capable of capturing one particular moment in time.

The *Ban Dainagon Ekotoba* (Pl. 2, Color Pl. 4), in three scrolls, tells the true story of a state minister, Tomo Ban no Yoshio, who in the Teikan era set fire to the Ōtemmon Gate in Kyoto and laid the blame on the Minister of the Left Minamoto no Makoto in an attempt to ruin him. The truth leaked out, however, and Yoshio himself was banished to a remote island. The story, thus, centers around the nobles serving at the court, but characters from the lower levels of society are also worked in, and their activities are given an importance equal to, if not greater than, those of the aristocracy.

Again, the same technique in drawing faces and the same "bird's-eye" views of interiors as in the *Genji* scrolls are used when the setting is the interior of the Minister of the Left's house, and the style used is that of the *tsukuri-e* with its heavy colors. In portraying the common people, however, free use is made of vigorous lines which bring out the liveliness of their movements. In one sense, then, the style of this *emaki* is a combination of those of the *Genji* and *Shigi-san* scrolls. The story, however, is like the *Shigi-san Engi* in laying more emphasis on action than, as do the *Genji* scrolls, on mood. Another point on which it resembles the former is that there are only four sections of text throughout the whole

5   *Ban Dainagon Ekotoba* (Detail)

three scrolls, the pictures showing a whole succession of varied incidents in unbroken succession. Yet again, though the work makes use of the *tsukuri-e* technique, it attempts to give a greater sense of movement to its heavily-painted figures (Fig. 5). This, together with its attempt to portray human beings more realistically, are sure signs of how the work is striving to open up new fields for the *emaki*.

It seems likely that the age produced other lively, realistic *emaki* of this kind. There are records, for example, of a four-scroll *Go-sannen Kassen Emaki* (Stories of the Go-sannen Civil War) (Color Pl. 5), which the painter Myōjitsu is said to have produced in 1171 at the command of the cloistered Emperor Goshirakawa. As the title shows, its subject was battles, and the appearance of this kind of scroll can be taken as further proof that the spirit of the new age, with its love of vigorous

# Plate 2

## The Complete First Scroll from *Ban Dainagon Ekotoba*

See page 171 for an explanation of *Ban Dainagon Ekotoba*.

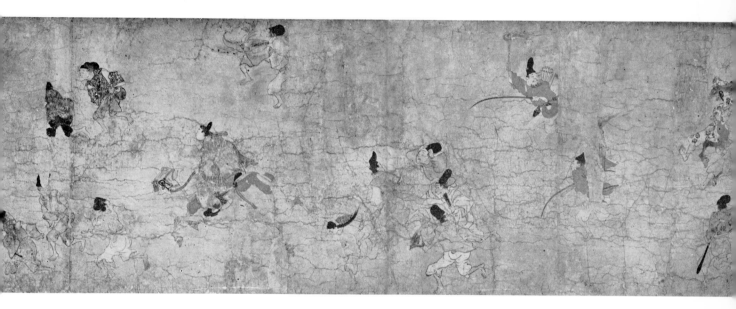

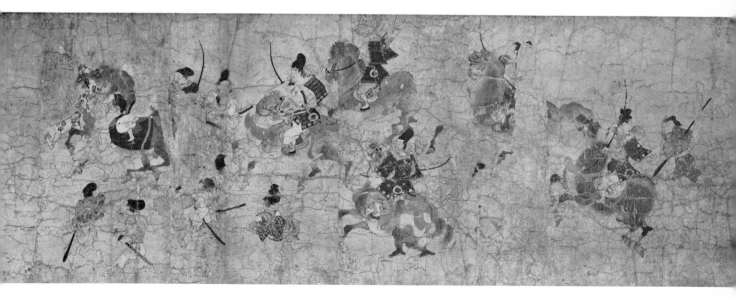

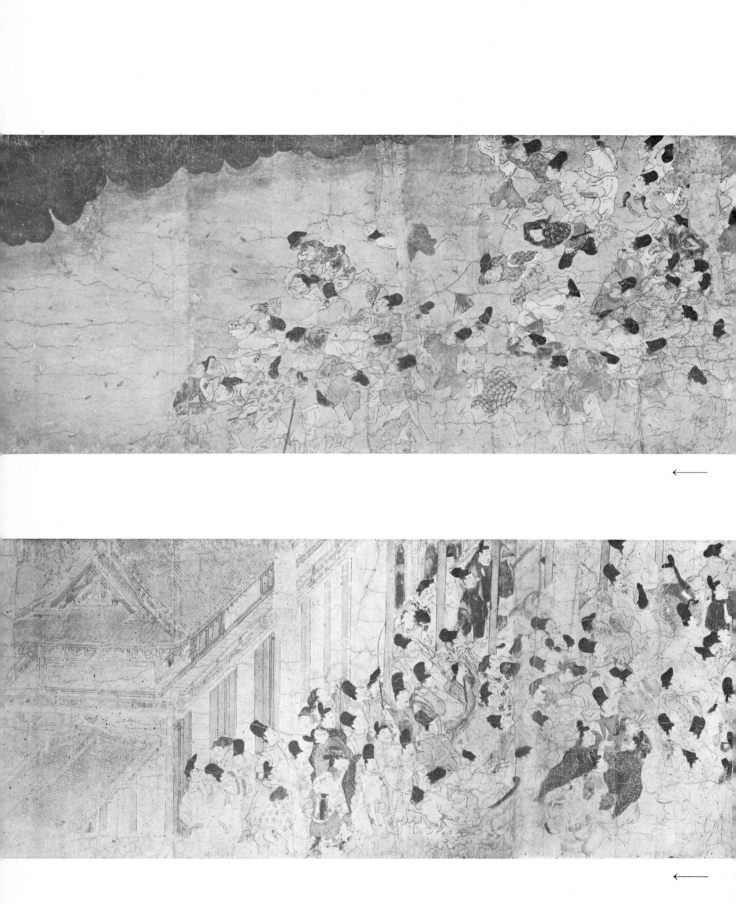

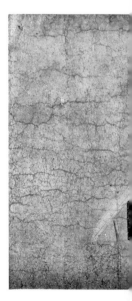

The above is the first scroll from *Ban Dainagon Ekotoba*. Most of the scroll is devoted to the fire at *Otemmon* (Oten Gate), but the last section shows the Dainagon falsely charging his political foe with arson. The story continues through scrolls two and three. Scrolls two and three contain narrative, but scroll one, as with *Shigisan Engi*, contains no narrative.

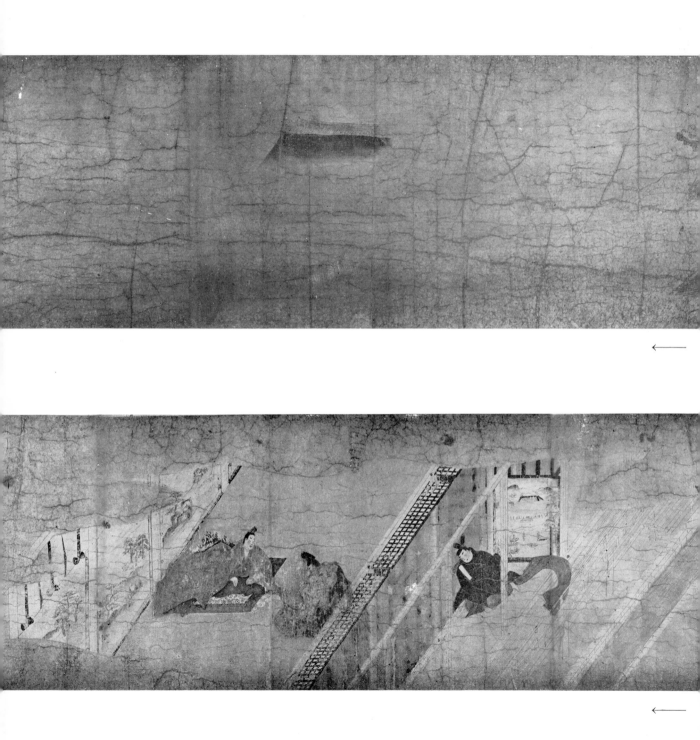

movement, was making itself felt in the *emaki*. The *Nenjū Gyōji E* (Annual Functions in the Imperial Court), in 60 scrolls—also made reportedly at the command of the Emperor Goshirakawa—was destroyed by fire, and all that we have today are copies of a dozen or so of the scrolls. Even so, they are enough to show how realistically the work portrayed customs of the time and how vividly, it portrayed human beings at their various activities. In this it bears certain resemblances to the *Ban Dainagon Ekotoba*. Again, the *Daijōe Misogi Gyōkō E,* no longer extant, was a large-scale work recording in seven scrolls the visit of the Emperor Rokujō in 1166 to a shrine for purification rites, and doubtless presented an objective account of events which had actually taken place. It is extremely significant that, alongside works such as the *Genji Monogatari Emaki* which relied solely on the evocation of particular moods, this new type of work should have been produced which showed such a strong concern for actualities.

One other work produced by this age that cannot be overlooked is the *Chōjū Giga* (Fig. 6), reportedly the work of Toba Sōjō. Four scrolls are extant, and these are generally known together as *Chōjū Giga,* but closer inspection reveals that their contents are all different in nature, and that the style is also inconsistent. The first scroll shows monkeys, hares, frogs, etc., amusing themselves by imitating human beings. The second shows the appearance and habits of various animals, including such imaginary beasts as the dragon and the unicorn. The third scroll falls in two parts; the first shows priests and laymen playing gambling games, the second shows monkeys, hares, and frogs amusing themselves imitating human beings. The fourth scroll is rather similar to the first half of the third, and is devoted chiefly to priests and laymen at play. All four scrolls are

in the *hakubyō* style, using black lines only. The first two are by the
same hand and are considered to be a product of this age (twelfth century)
but the two halves of the third scroll and the fourth scroll are all by
different artists, and are believed to have been produced after the beginning
of the Kamakura period, in the thirteenth century.

It is the first scroll that is generally familiar under the name *Chōjū
Giga;* it is also the best artistically. Two types of ink, thick and thin,
are employed. In comparison with the other scrolls, the brushwork is more
fluent, free, and varied, and the whole scroll is devoted to the frolickings
of the various animals, presented in one continuous, shifting scene without
a single word of text. In the mastery of the touch and the excellence of
the draftsmanship, the work unquestionably represents a peak among works
employing the *hakubyō* technique. And in its variety and humor it has—
despite differences of subject matter and style—something in common with

the *Shigi-san Engi* scroll, being typical of the new, more vital age that was coming.

Late Heian thus saw the *emaki* achieve an increasing diversity. Alongside the conservative, traditional works which were still being produced, other works, representative of the new social order, also began to put in their appearance. Where the one type strove after ever greater refinement in its beauty and the moods it evoked, the other showed a partiality for the comic, the vigorous, the realistic, and the miraculous. Where style was concerned also, the one followed slavishly the decorative *tsukuri-e* style which had been in vogue since middle Heian times, while the new school strove to capture the life inherent in all things by making use of individuality of line.

To sum up, the Heian period, which during the tenth and eleventh centuries succeeded in fashioning the purely Japanese picture

←

scroll, went on in the twelfth century to produce the four *emaki* master-pieces—the *Genji, Shigi-san, Ban Dainagon,* and *Chōjū Giga* scrolls—which form, one might say, the backbone of the form as a whole. In this sense, the late Heian period saw the form reach the highest artistic level in its history.

## The Kamakura Period (1185-1392)

As we have seen, the *emaki* toward the end of the Heian period became increasingly diversified in its subject matter. Now, with the beginning of the Kamakura period, we see this diversity increased still further, and the beginning of the period of the picture scroll's greatest popularity.

In one sense this diversity is only a reflection of the cultural and

*Chōjū Giga*

social complexity of the Kamakura period as a whole. Following the civil wars of Hogen and Heiji, the emergence of the Taira family brought a temporary calm to society, but with the succession of great historical events that were to follow shortly after—the fall of the Tairas and the establishment of the Kamakura Bakufu, followed by the collapse of the Minamotos and the disturbances of the Shōkyū era—it was once more plunged into chaos. The consequent disturbances in the social psychology and the changes wrought in the social order had a profound effect on the religion, culture, and emotional tenor of the age alike. And the complexity of the Kamakura culture that emerged as a result of the storms and stresses of the age, reflected in turn in the *emaki,* produced the unprecedented variety that we have just mentioned. Of the relationship between Kamakura culture as a whole and the Kamakura *emaki,* and of the special characteristics of the latter, we shall have more to say later. One can, however, sum up the new trends in one phrase—increased realism, a realism that was eloquent witness to the way the social upheavals of the day forced people to face up directly to cold reality.

The secular scrolls produced by the age are of many kinds, being variously based on romances, poems, legends and fables, war chronicles, and historical records.

First, there are those works which draw for their material on the romances and diaries of the Heian period (e.g., the *Genji Monogatari, Sagoromo Monogatari, Nezame Monogatari, Eiga Monogatari,* and *Murasaki Shikibu Nikki*), or on the neo-classical literature of the Kamakura period (e.g., the *Matsuura Monogatari, Sumiyoshi Monogatari,* and *Torikaebaya Monogatari*). The number of these works extant today, or whose names are known from old records, is considerable. The aristocracy of the age, though its authority had fallen into the hands of the warriors and its everyday life was becoming increasingly less romantic, still persisted in producing this kind of romantic work—a sign, perhaps, not only of the traditional conservatism of the court noble but also of his defiance of the newly arisen warrior class before which he had succumbed. The aristocracy's impotence in actual society only served to increase the respect and nostalgia it felt for the glories of Heian, a respect which manifested itself in a reverence for tradition in learning and the arts, and in the worship of the classics. The *Genji Monogatari,* as popular as ever among the aristocracy, was now read with something approaching a religious fervor.

It is only natural that a type of *emaki* should have been produced that corresponded with this taste in literature. This type of scroll would seem to have been particularly in evidence in the period following the

7    *Murasaki Shikibu Nikki Emaki*

Shōkyū disturbances (1221), and around the age of the Emperor Godaigo (1318-1339), when the tendency to hark back to the past was particularly strong. Scrolls extant today such as the *Murasaki Shikibu Nikki Emaki* (Lady Murasaki's Diary) (Fig. 7), *Monogatari Emaki, Komakurabe Gyōkō Emaki* (Story of an Imperial Visit to the Horse Race), *Sagoromo Monogatari Emaki*, and *Sumiyoshi Monogatari Emaki* (Tales of Sumiyoshi) mostly adopt the *tsukuri-e* form of the previous age, and it seems likely that the different versions of the *Genji* and *Sagoromo* stories and the many other scrolls of this type known today only by name were also in the same style.

As far as one can judge from extant specimens, however, this type of scroll became increasingly less artistic as the age progressed, and the old charm and lyricism to be found, say, in the *Genji Monogatari* scroll eventually disappeared completely. The scrolls, in fact, are no more

8  *Sanjūroku Kasen Emaki*

than an attempt to recapture, in the mind alone, a grace and elegance
that had vanished from actual society.  They are products of the brain,
divorced from the true essence of romanticism.  They reveal the conservative
and traditional tastes of the nobility of the age, without demonstrating any
of the new aspects that developed in the picture scroll during the Kamakura period.

The background of the series of picture scrolls based on *waka,*
31-syllable poems, is similarly the old culture of the nobility, yet they are
worthy of note for a new creativity typical of the age.  The *waka,* even
during this period, still retained its traditional sway over the court nobles;
a large variety of Imperial anthologies and collections of individual poets'
works were compiled—among them the celebrated *Shin-kokinshū*—while there
was a great vogue for *uta-awase,* or poetical contests.  This trend also led
to the idolization of celebrated poets of old, who were known as *kasen,*
or "sages of poetry."  The *kasen emaki, uta-awase emaki* and other similar
picture scrolls peculiar to this period were all produced under the stimulus
of this boom in poetry.

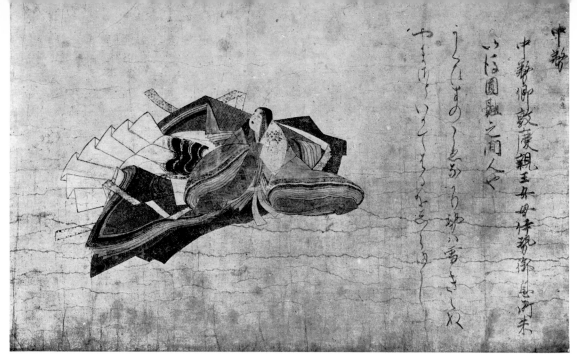

9　*Sanjūroku Kasen Emaki*

The picture scroll dealing with women poets from the *Kokinshū* and two other famous anthologies of *waka,* which the *Azuma-Kagami* records as having been presented to the Shōgun Minamoto no Sanetomo in 1213, was a massive work comprising 20 scrolls in all. According to the record, it was a collection of illustrations to the poems, and to the prefaces in which the circumstances under which each poem was composed were described. Nothing is known of the style of painting, but it is worthy of note as a product of the early Kamakura period, when poetry contests were extremely popular, and for the large number of scrolls of which it was composed.

A number of these scrolls depicting celebrated poets of old are extant today, one of the most celebrated being the *Sanjūroku Kasen Emaki* (Portraits of Thirty-six Famous Poets) (Fig. 8, Color Pl. 10). They all consist of portraits of the 36 "poetical sages" or other famous poets, accompanied by specimens of their works. In the case of the Satake version of the *Sanjūroku Kasen Emaki,* the celebrated poets with whom it deals— Kakinomoto no Hitomaro, the poetess Nakatsukasa (Fig. 9) and the like—

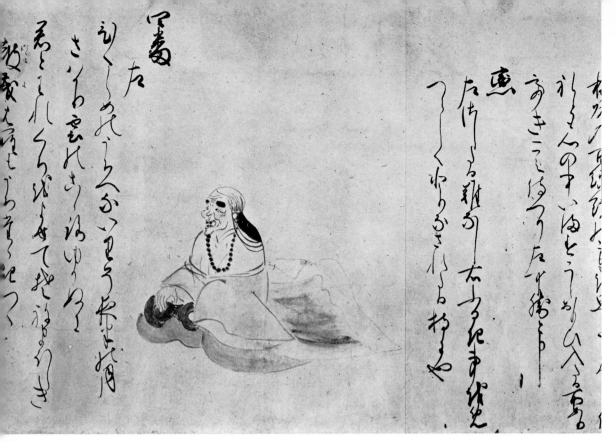

10　*Tōhoku-in Shokunin Uta-awase Emaki*

all lived long before the time the scroll was produced, yet the faces in the pictures all show a sufficient individuality to justify the name of "portraits." In fact, it is the individuality and realism with which the poets are portrayed that constitutes the principal esthetic value of the scroll. This is an extremely important point, and the tendency toward realism here demonstrated is noteworthy as one of the chief characteristics of the *emaki* during the Kamakura period.

Surviving "poetry contest scrolls" include the *Tōhoku-in Shokunin Uta-awase Emaki,* the *Jidai Fudō Uta-awase,* and the *Ise Shin-Meisho Uta-awase Emaki.* The poems in the *Tōhoku-in Shokunin Uta-awase Emaki* (Fig. 10) are by members of professions such as doctor, smith, swordgrinder, shrine maiden, and founder, while in the *Jidai Fudō Uta-awase* they are by celebrated poets such as Hitomaro, Komachi, Semimaru and Nōin Hōshi.

The pairs of poets whose works were judged together are placed side by side, and their works are inscribed alongside the portraits. The pictures in the *Ise Shin-Meisho Uta-awase Emaki* (Fig. 11) are of a new set of "ten scenic spots" near the Ise Shrine, which were selected as the subject for a poetry contest.

The appearance, as main themes in these scrolls, of landscapes pure and simple and of ordinary working people shows that new fields were being opened up for the *emaki*. A particularly important innovation is the way the *Tōhoku-in Shokunin Uta-awase Emaki* treats its working people as a subject in their own right, and not merely as unimportant adjuncts to other things.

The predominance of an aristocratic, romantic literature in the Heian period had been accompanied at the same time by the beginnings of a more popular literature—the *Konjaku Monogatari*, for instance—which relied chiefly on legends and fables for its subject-matter. With the Kamakura period, now, there appeared a whole succession of collections in the same style as the *Konjaku Monogatari,* among them the *Uji Shūi Monogatari* and the *Kokōn Chomonshū*. This literary trend was paralleled in the field of *emaki* by the appearance of scrolls based on colorful or fantastic legends

12   *Yamai no Sōshi*

or on real life.   In this category can be included works such as the *Yamai no Sōshi* (Scroll of Diseases and Deformities), the *Kibi Daijin Nittō Ekotoba* (Story of Minister Kibi's Trip to China), the *Eshi no Sōshi* (Story of a Painter), and the *Obusuma Saburō Ekotoba* (Story of the Warrior Obusuma Saburō).

The *Yamai no Sōshi* (Fig. 12) gives details of strange diseases and deformities to be encountered in various parts of the country.   The pictures, while completely realistic in their portrayal of these more repulsive aspects of humanity, at the same time bring to bear on them a kind of ironic humor.   The scroll is sometimes classified along with religious works such as the *Jigoku Zōshi* and *Gaki Zōshi* (to be mentioned later), since human ills were always considered at the time in the light of Buddhist ideas of *karma* and reincarnation.   It is equally possible, however, to see it simply as a vivid piece of secular reporting on actual life at the time.

13   *Eshi no Sōshi*

The *Eshi no Sōshi* (Fig. 13) tells, with humorous touches, the
tragic tale of the sufferings of a poverty-stricken teacher of painting.   Like
the *Yamai no Sōshi*, it would seem to be based on real life.

The setting of the *Obusuma Saburō Ekotoba* (Fig. 14) is a warrior
home in the Kantō district, and the scroll covers, with a certain degree of
religious coloring, a whole range of subjects—fighting, love affairs, cruel
stepmothers, and the like.   This too was probably based on real-life events.

The *Kibi Daijin Nittō Ekotoba* tells a highly colorful tale of how
the minister Kibi no Makibi visits T'ang China and is asked all kinds of

14   *Obusuma Saburō Ekotoba*

difficult questions, intended to test his talent, by the court there. He encounters the spirit of Abe no Nakamaro, and with its aid comes through the tests successfully.

These picture scrolls, thus, are quite varied in their subject matter. They are alike, however, in showing the same Buddhistic and plebeian leanings, the same love of the strange and fantastic, as the legendary literature of the day, and in containing new elements unknown to the romances of the previous age. Moreover, one detects in works such as the *Yamai no Sōshi* and the *Eshi no Sōshi* something of the humor and pathos of actuality; the romantic effect aimed at by literature of the *Genji* type is replaced by the pursuit of truth, by the desire to come to grips with the grim realities of this world. The number of such works extant, however, is small, nor are there many records of other works apparently in the same category. It thus seems likely that the genre remained comparatively

16    *Mōko Shūrai Ekotoba*

unexploited in the Kamakura period and that its only influence was on the *otogi-zōshi* scrolls of the following Muromachi age, to which its elements of the fantastic appealed.

We have already seen how at the end of the Heian period there appeared scrolls such as the *Go-sannen Kassen Emaki,* which told the story of famous battles.    Now, with the establishment of the Kamakura military government, this type of scroll became increasingly popular.    This was only a natural parallel to a similar trend in literature, which saw a sudden spate of martial pieces—the *Hogen Monogatari, Heiji Monogatari, Heike Monogatari,* and *Gempei Seisuiki* among them.    The historical work *Azuma Kagami* tells how Minamoto no Sanetomo in 1204 ordered a Kyoto painter to produce the *MasakadoKassen Emaki,* while in 1210 he ordered from Kyoto the *Ōshū Jūninen Kassen Emaki.*    The only works in this category extant from the Kamakura period are the *Heiji Monogatari Emaki* (Stories of the Heiji Civil War), the *Mōko Shūrai Ekotoba* (Stories of the Mongol Invasion), the *Go-sannen Kassen Emaki,* and the *Zen-kunen Kassen Emaki,* but the number actually produced was probably far greater.

Prominent among the *emaki* on martial themes is the *Heiji Mono-*

17  *Zuishin Teiki Emaki*

*gatari Emaki* (Fig. 15, Color Pl. 11) which tells of the civil strife of the Heiji era. In particular, the version in the possession of the National Museum in Tokyo serves, in its delicate lines and exquisite colorings, as a model of what the *yamato-e* should be. The *Mōko Shūrai Ekotoba* (Fig. 16), on the other hand, is coarse in its brushwork and lacks finesse. It seems, however, that the Takezaki Suenaga who ordered the work, related his experiences in fighting the Mongol invader directly to the artist, so that his own exploits could be recorded for posterity. As a result, the battle scenes have a vividness and authenticity absent from other similar scrolls, which record battles of the more distant past.

Alongside the "martial" *emaki* stands what may be called the "documentary" *emaki,* which records events of historical importance or presents portraits of documentary significance. Scrolls in this category still-

extant include the *Chūden Gyokai Zukan,* the *Zuishin Teiki Emaki* (Imperial Guard Cavalry) (Fig. 17), the *Tennō Sekkan Daijin Ei Zukan,* and the *Kuge Retsuei Zukan* (Fig. 18).   All are in the nature of commemorative group portraits, the faces of the Emperor and the court nobles being painted with a realistic touch that gives each a high degree of individuality.

The *Chūden Gyokai Zukan* (the extant version is a copy) was reputedly the work of Fujiwara Nobuzane, while *Tennō Sekkan Daijin Ei Zukan* is said to be by Tamenobu and Gōshin, in the same family line as Nobuzane.   Nobuzane, active in early Kamakura times, was the leading exponent of the *nise-e,* or portrait in the *yamato-e* style, and founded his own school of portrait-painters.   A number of other extant works, including the *Sanjūroku Kasen Emaki,* are attributed to him.

The birth of this type of *emaki* in this period was of course due

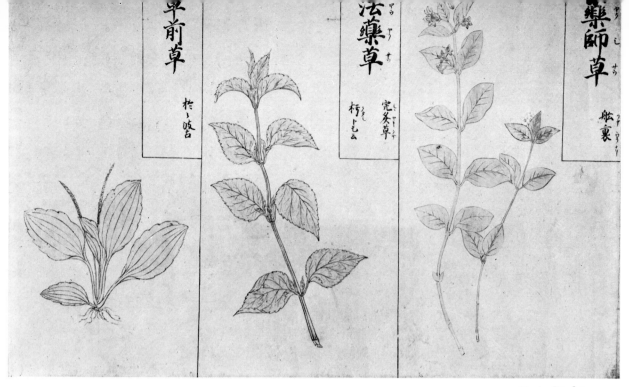

車前草　　　法藥草　　　藥師草

19　*Bai Sōshi*

in part to the appearance of artists such as Nobuzane. However, it was also a result of the new spirit of realism and objectivity, a spirit which created an interest in the individualistic presentation of human beings and a demand for likeness in their portraits. The same approach was extended to animals and plants also. A number of scrolls are still extant—among them the *Sungyū Ekotoba,* the *Bai Sōshi* (Scroll of Veterinary Gods and Herbs), and the *Zuishin Teiki Emaki*—which include astonishingly realistic paintings of horses and cows, while there are equally faithful pictures of various herbs at the end of the *Bai Sōshi* (Fig. 19).

The works mentioned so far are all secular in content, but the Kamakura period also saw a remarkable development in the religious picture scroll. We have seen, it is true, earlier examples of works of a Buddhistic nature—the *E Inga-kyō* of the Nara period and the *Shigi-san Engi* of the Heian period, for instance—but these were not enough to constitute a tradition. It was not until the Kamakura period that the religious picture scroll acquired a position where it could vie with its secular counterpart.

90

20  *Kegon Gojūgo-sho Emaki*

The new religions of the Kamakura period were a product of the social unrest and upheavals of the late Heian and early Kamakura periods, and of the decadence of the existing religious order. Under their stimulus, the Tendai and Shingon sects and the six sects of Nara also experienced a great revival. In the new atmosphere of religious activity thus created, the different sects vied with each other in publicizing the miraculous events associated with their temples and the achievements of the famous priests they had produced. To this end, they made great use of the *emaki,* which is one of the main reasons for the sudden development of the religious picture scroll at this period.

The subject matter of the religious picture scroll, however, was varied, and besides the types just mentioned there were others which reflected the religious pessimism of the day or which satirized the overbearing ways of the clergy. Among scrolls based directly or indirectly on the scriptures, there were the *Kegon Gojūgo-sho Emaki* (Zenzai Doji's Pilgrimage to Fifty-five Saints), the *Jūni Innen Emaki,* the *Jigoku Zōshi* (Scroll of Hells), and the *Gaki Zōshi* (Scroll of Hungry Ghosts). These are all pictorial illustrations of religious texts. The *Kegon Gojūgo-sho Emaki* (Fig. 20), along with

the *Kegon Engi* mentioned later, bears witness to the revival of the Kegon sect in the early Kamakura period.    The *Jigoku Zōshi* (Fig. 21, Color Pl. 6) and *Gaki Zōshi* (Fig. 22, Color Pl. 7) are both based on the Buddhist idea of the transmigration of souls between the Six Realms.   The former shows the unremitting torments suffered by those who have fallen into Hell, while the latter shows the weird *gaki*, or "hungry ghosts," under-going the torments of their own particular realm.

Both the two latter works, though cruel and uncompromising, conceal an ironic touch not without flashes of a kind of humor.   These scrolls are typical products of the belief prevailing at the time that the Latter Day of the Law, as predicted by the Buddha, had arrived—a con-

22  *Gaki Zōshi*

viction born of the social upheavals and uncertainty of the late Heian and early Kamakura years. The despair and disgust with their present life engendered by this uncertainty drove men to faith in the Pure Land of the new Buddhist sects, and these scrolls would seem to have been produced partly with the aim of heightening longing for this Pure Land still further, by exposing the evils of the present world and the terrors of the transmigration cycle. The realistic outlook of the age can again be seen in the literalness with which the horrors of hell and the grotesqueness of the *gaki* are depicted.

Such scrolls based on the scriptures were produced chiefly in the early Kamakura period, and saw little subsequent development. On the

other hand, scrolls relating the histories of temples or shrines, miraculous events associated with them, or the lives of celebrated priests enjoyed a great vogue from now on.

The temple history had already existed since Nara times. In late Heian, it came to have literary significance and then to be joined with pictures in the form of *emaki*. However, it was not until the Kamakura period that the form attained its full development and popularity. In this period, laymen in general came to look to pictures for their religious knowledge. Moreover, as we have already seen, the religious forms of early Kamakura led to rivalry among the sects in presenting the special claims of their own temples. For this purpose, the *emaki,* as they realized, was ideally suited.

Many different works in this category are extant. Three of the most famous are the *Kokawa-dera Engi* (Legends of Kokawa-dera Temple), the *Taima Mandara Engi* (Legends of the Taima Mandara) (Fig. 23), and the *Ishiyama-dera Engi* (Legends of Ishiyama-dera Temple) (Fig. 24). The actual number produced must have been incomparably greater. Besides works on Buddhist temples, a considerable number of scrolls were also

24  *Ishiyama-dera Engi*

produced which dealt with Shinto shrines—telling, for example, how the particular god first came to be worshipped there, or relating miraculous events associated with the shrine. Among the considerable number still extant are the celebrated "Shōkyū" version of the *Kitano Tenjin Engi* (Legends of Kitano Tenjin Shrine) (Fig. 25, Color Pl. 9) and the other "Tenjin Engi" which it inspired; the *Sannō Reigen Ki;* the *Kasuga Gongen Reigen Ki* (Legends of the Kasuga Gongen Miracles) (Fig. 26); and others.

Even more prolifically produced than this kind of scroll was the *emaki* based on biographies of the founders of sects or of other celebrated priests, inspired partly by reverence for its heroes and partly by sectarian rivalry. Biographies of Dengyō Daishi and Kōbō Daishi had already appeared, written in quasi-Chinese, during the Heian period, but it was not till the Kamakura period that such works first became popular in *emaki* form. The newly-appeared Pure Land schools of Buddhism produced many works of this new type, among them the *Hōnen Shōnin Eden* (Biography of Saint Hōnen) (Fig. 27), the *Shinran Shōnin Eden,* and the *Ippen Shōnin Eden* (Color Pl. 12). The other sects also produced

25 *Kitano Tenjin Engi*

many similar works, among them *Kegon Engi* (History of Kegon Buddhism) (Fig. 28, Color Pl. 8) of the Kegon Sect, the *Hossō-shū Hiji Ekotoba* of the Hossō Sect, the *Tōsei Eden* (The Journey East) (Fig. 29) of the Ritsu Sect, and the *Kōbō Daishi Eden* of the Shingon Sect. This kind of work continued to be produced after the end of the Kamakura period, and many of these scroll have survived to this day, while many others now known only by name must also have been produced in the Kamakura period.

The new sects such as the Jōdo, Shin, and Ji sects were popular

26 *Kasuga Gongen Reigen Ki*

27 *Hōnen Shōnin Eden*

27   *Hōnen Shōnin Eden*

forms of Buddhism, and their founders, in order to spread their teachings, ranged far from the towns into remote country districts. Their biographies, accordingly, contain a considerable amount of local color—country scenes, as well as the customs and daily habits of warriors, farmers, and other ordinary people in the provinces. Particularly in the case of works produced soon after the death of the priests with whom they dealt, the need to make the settings and facts authentic resulted in a considerable degree of realism in the portrayal of nature and social conditions. This trend, which is also discernible in the temple and shrine histories discussed above, represents a new field opened up by the religious *emaki* of this period.

Production of these religious works increased still more with time, and the number of scrolls to each individual work also grew. The *Kitano Tenjin Engi* (Shōkyū version), for example, has nine scrolls, the *Ippen Shōnin Eden* and *Hossō-shū Hiji Ekotoba* 12 each, and the *Kasuga Gongen Reigen Ki* 20, while the *Hōnen Shōnin Eden* has as many as 48.

So far we have concentrated chiefly on the subject matter of the

97

Kamakura-period picture scroll. Let us now briefly consider the style. In the early part of the period, the two basic styles represented by the *Genji Monogatari Emaki* and the *Shigi-san Engi* were followed faithfully. As the age progressed, however, the distinction between the two became blurred and various compromise styles appeared.

For example, the *Murasaki Shikibu Nikki Emaki,* considered to be a product of the early Kamakura period, together with other works based on the lyrical literature of Heian days, sticks faithfully to the *tsukuri-e* style, while religious works such as the *Kokawa-dera Engi, Jigoku Zōshi,* and *Gaki Zōshi* adhere more or less to the emphasis on line seen in the *Shigi-san Engi.* The clear-cut distinction gradually disappears, however. The "Shōkyū" version of the *Kitano Tenjin Engi,* for example, which belongs to the earlier part of the period, is a powerful work which combines a bold, resilient use of line with an emphasis on rich colors. The mid-Kamakura *Heiji Monogatari Emaki* achieves an effect of nobility by blending rich colors with delicacy of line, while the *Saigyō Monogatari Emaki* (Fig. 30), *Kitano Tenjin Engi* (Kōan version), and *Ise Shin-Meisho Uta-awase Emaki* have a mild elegance effected by a combination of fine lines and pale colors. The twenty volumes of the *Kasuga Gongen Reigen Ki* which, toward the end of the period, achieved the technical consummation of the Kamakura *emaki,* afford a kind of comprehensive survey of

29    *Tōsei Eden*

*emaki* technique during the period, and are considered to have provided the basis of the style of the later Tosa school of painting.

Thus on the one hand color and line were being combined experimentally in a whole variety of techniques and forms. On the other hand, however, picture scrolls such as the *Zuishin Teiki Emaki,* the *Chūden Gyokai Zukan,* and the *Makura no Sōshi Emaki* (The Pillow Book) (Fig. 31) were being produced in the *hakubyō* style, which relies almost entirely on the India ink line and uses next to no color at all. Nor can one overlook the invasion of the *emaki* field by the Chinese styles of painting of the Sung and Yüan periods. This is particularly evident in works such as the *Kegon Engi, Kibi Daijin Nittō Ekotoba, Jōdo Goso Eden,* and *Tōsei Eden,* which are largely set in foreign countries. The Chinese styles are different from those hitherto used in the picture scroll— in their use of shades for trees, rocks and embankments, for instance, and in their use of color—and their subsequent influence is too important to be overlooked.

To sum up, the chief features of the picture scroll in the Kamakura period were the richness of its content, the increased range of its

←

subject matter, the increase in its length, and the diversity of styles it employed. A medieval outlook that strove to follow the traditions of the previous age remained a persistent underlying force, yet on the other hand new elements were appearing, elements which reflected the more realistic bent of the up-and-coming warrior society. These, together with the great development occasioned by reforms in the religious world, gave the *emaki* in this period a very great variety of content, a variety matched by the diversity of the styles employed. There was a gradual change from the decorative to the descriptive, from the romantic to the realistic, and a new emphasis came to be placed on individuality and objectivity.

Again, as a result of the increasing diversity of subject matter, the types of characters portrayed were extended to include not only Japanese but Chinese and Koreans, not only aristocrats but people in every conceiva-

ble walk of life—from priests, warriors, farmers, fishermen and artisans right down to prostitutes and beggars. An increasingly plebeian taste in the choice of subject matter is another conspicuous feature. The range of human experience covered is wide—love, battle, labor and religion, the noble, the repulsive, the tragic, the comic and the elegant. The physical output increased correspondingly; the *emaki* came to be used to a remarkable extent not merely for esthetic but for religious purposes also, and in the Kamakura period achieved a popularity unparalleled in its history.

## The Muromachi Period (1392 - 1573)

The political struggle which had been going on between the court nobles and the samurai, based in Kyoto and Kamakura respectively, ended

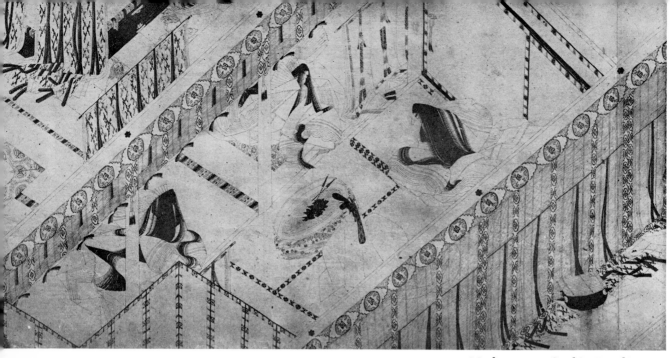

with the capitulation of the court nobles. The political and economic decline of the *kuge* and the strengthening of the power of the samurai was particularly marked after the struggle between the Northern and Southern dynasties, and this had its effect in turn on Japanese culture as a whole. Especially during the time from the establishment of the Muromachi Bakufu by the Ashikaga family until the latter part of the fourteenth century, the samurai who had made their way into Kyoto gradually matured culturally. They began to imitate the courtiers in their daily lives and became increasingly well versed in the courtly culture. From this period, the court culture which had so long reigned supreme became less and less important and a new warrior culture—based on the old court culture but adding to it new qualities peculiar to the samurai class—began to take over. Moreover, the same period saw an increase in the influence of the Zen sect, which became closely bound up with the samurai class, and a stepping-up of trade with the mainland, which meant the introduction of cultural elements from Yüan and Ming China. The so-called "Higashi-yama" culture of the late fifteenth century, and of the age of Ashikaga Yoshimasa in particular, is typical of the samurai culture that resulted from this mixture of different elements.

The 20-scroll *Kasuga Gongen Reigen Ki* produced in 1309, a mighty achievement typical of the Kamakura period, had been a kind of consummation and summing-up of the whole of that period. At the same time, the originality apparent in the works of Heian and early Kamakura times had already almost completely disappeared; the style had become stiff and stereotyped, and the content increasingly devoid of any artistic inspiration. The tendency toward stereotyped techniques and the diminishing emphasis on composition became still more marked in the Muromachi period. The decline in the *emaki* was accompanied by a strong fashion for painting in the styles of Sung and Yuan, and this fashion, by weakening the position of the *yamato-e,* helped on still further the decline of a form of which this *yamato-e* formed the basic style.

The Sung and Yüan styles were brought into Japan along with Zen Buddhism. At first, works in this style were to be found only in Zen monasteries, but in time they became extremely popular among the warrior clans who patronized Zen. At the same time, there appeared from the ranks of the Zen priesthood a succession of painters specializing in the Sung- and Yüan-style India ink painting (for example, Shūbun and and Sesshū). Gradually the painters drew away from the influence of the Zen sect, and eventually there appeared schools such as the Kanō school, painting Nipponized "Chinese pictures" which aimed chiefly at satisfying the artistic tastes of the samurai.

These Sung- and Yüan-style paintings received such enthusiastic support from the warrior class that within a short space of time they reigned supreme in the field of Muromachi art, and the power of the already-declining *yamato-e* and *emaki* inevitably dwindled still further.

Under such conditions as these, picture scrolls based on the classical romances and on *waka* poetry such as were produced in the Kamakura period disappeared almost completely. During the Kamakura period the court nobles were still superior, culturally at least, and nostalgic works based on the classics continued to appear. With the Muromachi period, however, the nobles lost even this remaining degree of vitality and produced nothing new at all. Even after this, roughly throughout the fifteenth century, *emaki* were still popular at court and among the Bakufu gentry, as is clear from diaries of the period. The number of devotees was extremely small, however, and even these in their turn disappeared from mid-Muromachi times on.

The heyday of the *emaki* designed for purely esthetic enjoyment thus ended with the Kamakura period. With the Muromachi period, this type of scroll sought to explore new fields by telling stories in pictures based on material of the kind found in the *otogi-zōshi*. These *otogi-zōshi,* which were very popular, were short tales with a moral, sometimes resembling fairy tales and aimed at the very young, the very old, and women. They relied for their material on various kinds of tales and legends, their heroes ranging from court nobles and warriors to priests, the common people, and even to birds, beasts and plants. Their chief characteristic, however, was that they always portrayed things from a plebeian point of view.

Many different kinds of scrolls were produced with such subject matter, the most famous including the *Fukutomi Zōshi* (Story of Fukutomi), the *Bakemono Zōshi,* the *Bukkigun Emaki,* and the *Tawara Tōta Emaki.* In style, some of these works are in the *yamato-e* tradition but, like the subject matter, the style is in most cases tasteless, unrefined, and clumsy. Even so, they do have a certain pleasing freedom from formal restraints. The best example of this type of *emaki* is the *Fukutomi Zōshi* (Fig. 32), which tells the story of an old man called Hidetake, who became prosperous solely on account of his prodigious ability at farting, and of the aged Fukutomi, who tried to imitate him and failed. Though the subject matter is comic and ribald in the extreme, the work has a quality of compelling realism, and there is something true to life underlying the humor.

An interesting characteristic of the *Fukutomi Zōshi,* one shared by many of the *otogi-zōshi* scrolls of the Muromachi period, is that there is no separate space for the text, the story being told in the form of a dialogue written in by the side of the speakers in the picture. This kind

33  *Yūzū Nembutsu Engi*

of *emaki* was aimed above all at the story-loving lower classes and differed enormously from the aristocratic, high-brow, and lyrical works found among the purely esthetic *emaki* of the past.  Possibly the vulgarization of this type of *emaki* and the loss of its traditions made the scroll form no longer suitable to the content, for the *otogi-zōshi* scroll soon gave way to the *nara-e-bon,* a kind of painted picture-book.

On the other hand, religious scrolls based on temple and shrine histories and the biographies of celebrated priests continued to be produced as ever, typical examples being the *Yūzū Nembutsu Engi* (Stories of the Origin of Yūzū Nembutsu Buddhism) (Fig. 33), the *Kōbō Daishi Ekotoba,* the *Kiyomizu-dera Engi* (Legends of Kiyomizu-dera Temple) (Fig. 34), and the *Hachiman-gū Engi.*  Unlike the non-religious scroll, the Muromachi religious scroll can be regarded as an extension of its Kamakura counterpart. Among extant examples, the *Yūzū Nembutsu Engi* in the Seiryō-ji is the best.  Produced by the best painters available in the official Bureau of Painting at the time, it carries on the old *yamato-e* tradition in its richness and delicacy.  Nevertheless, the style is formalized and has lost its life.

After this, religious scrolls became progressively cruder in style, settling eventually into an extremely rigid manner that incorporated elements from Chinese painting.  The decay of the *yamato-e* and the onslaught from Sung and Yüan styles that we have already mentioned ended by ruining the religious scroll esthetically in the same way as its secular counterpart.

Mitsunobu, the celebrated painter of the Tosa school who flourished at the time of the *emaki's* decline, is said to have produced many scrolls. Among them are the still extant *Kiyomizu-dera Engi,* the *Seikō-ji Engi,* and the *Kitano Tenjin Engi*. For all his celebrity, though, he was unable to give the form a new lease of life.

The *Seiryō-ji Engi* (Legends of Seiryō-ji Temple) (Fig. 35), a later work (c. 1515) reputedly by Kano Motonobu, differs from previous *yamato-e*-style scrolls in using Chinese techniques with a *yamato-e* flavor. It doubtless represented an innovation at the time it was produced, but its stilted Chinese effect and the absence of the elegance to be found in the old *emaki* prevented it from halting the decline of the form. And with the *Dōjō-ji Engi* (Legends of Dōjō-ji Temple) (Fig. 36), apparently a product of late Muromachi times, the dignity of the religious picture scroll has given way to a vulgarity reminiscent of the *otogi-zoshi* scrolls.

Thus while the religious scroll still continued to be produced, it

34  *Kiyomizu-dera Engi*

reached the same technical impasse as its secular counterpart, degenerating into a series of simple illustrations.   It is interesting to note here that from the end of the Kamakura period there began to appear *kakefuku* illustrating the histories of temples and shrines or the lives of famous clerics.

In form, the *kakefuku* resembled a hanging scroll on which a number of consecutive sections from an *emaki* had been pasted one below the other.   By its nature, the *emaki* was unsuitable for evangelizing large numbers of people, and the appearance of the *kakefuku* is in one way a witness to the changing needs of the times.   Just how far this new form helped encourage the decline of the religious picture scroll is not clear, but it remains true that in the Muromachi period the latter reached a dead end in the same way as the non-religious scroll, and that production virtually ceased.

The Japanese *emaki,* which had first appeared in mid-Heian times under the stimulus of the courtly romances, developed in close conjunction with the *yamato-e,* thanks to the support of the court nobles, the samurai, and the temples and shrines.   In the Muromachi period, it was forced into a decline by the decline of the *yamato-e* and by the loss of its former

patrons. By its very nature it was meant for leisurely appreciation, an ideal art form for an unhurried, aristocratic culture. In the new, harassed, and poor popular culture that grew up subsequently the *emaki* had no real place, and it was destined to be replaced sooner or later by books, *kakefuku*, or the like. Thus the *otogi-zōshi* scrolls gave way to the *nara-e-bon* with their painted illustrations, and then to the books of prints so popular among the masses of the Edo period, while the religious scrolls found a competitor in the new *kakefuku*.

Again, the inseparable dependence of the *emaki* on literature was a further weakness. The new Sung and Yüan styles of painting which came into Japan incidentally to the import of Zen Buddhism, and particularly the Chinese-style landscapes, taught the Japanese the delights of painting purely for its own sake—to the detriment of the picture scroll. And with the subsequent replacing of the religious *emaki* by the *kakefuku*, the victory of the painting in *kakemono* form was complete.

With this, then, the history of the Japanese picture scroll came to an end. Occasional works in scroll form were, and are, still produced— some of them by famous masters—but they neither attempt nor achieve anything new where the methods of composition peculiar to the *emaki* are concerned, and they lack almost entirely the interest inherent in the picture scroll proper. When all is said and done, the fate of the form was irretrievably bound up with that of the *yamato-e,* and the death of the latter in the Muromachi period meant the death to all intents and purposes of the *emaki* also.

# Composition

THE *emaki* is painted and written on a scroll, which means that the space available has very little height but very great length. The height ranges from 21.81 cm. (*Genji Monogatari Emaki*) to 52.12 cm., the usual height being from about 30 cm. to 40 cm. The length, however, is very variable; the longest may reach, as in the case of the *Kibi Daijin Nittō Ekotoba,* as much as 24.4 meters for one scroll. The usual length, however, is from 9 to 12 meters. The most common number of scrolls per work is two or three, but there are some of twenty scrolls or more, while one massive work, the *Hōnen Shōnin Eden* in the Chion-in, has 48 scrolls. The latter has a total length of 521.2 meters, which almost certainly makes it the longest in the world.

These physical characteristics of the picture scroll naturally mean that it requires a different approach from other art forms. Hanging scrolls, screens, and painted sliding doors, for instance, are viewed as a whole from a certain distance, and they are normally hung or placed so that they are perpendicular to the floor. The *emaki,* however, is placed flat on the table, and is viewed from above, in a leisurely fashion, the viewer unrolling the scroll with his left hand and rolling it up with his right.

Here are two of the form's most important characteristics—that it is held for viewing close to the viewer's own person, and that time is required in the viewing. (Two reasons, incidentally, why the practice of displaying one section at a time in a museum case is undesirable.) A form with such special characteristics can obviously handle different types of subject matter in a different manner from other forms. The long, horizontal space available makes possible development in both space and time. This possibility of development is, in fact, the most fundamental feature of the *emaki,* one which gives it a resemblance in some ways to the modern movie. This same possibility means that the most suitable subject matter is the varied affairs of the human world and narratives based on these affairs. Such subjects, indeed, account for the greater number of all *emaki,* a fact which shows how well the artists who made them appreciated the inherent possibilities of the form.

What follows is an account of how the picture scroll handles its material in relation to the possibilities offered and limitations imposed by this unique medium.

Deceived by the term "picture scroll," many people do not realize that almost all Japanese scrolls are made up of both pictures and text. The two are complementary and inseparable, the pictures explaining the text and the text supplementing the pictures. Scrolls entirely devoid of text, such as the *Chōjū Giga,* are rare exceptions; while the first scrolls of the *Shigi-san Engi* and *Ban Dainagon Ekotoba,* neither of which has

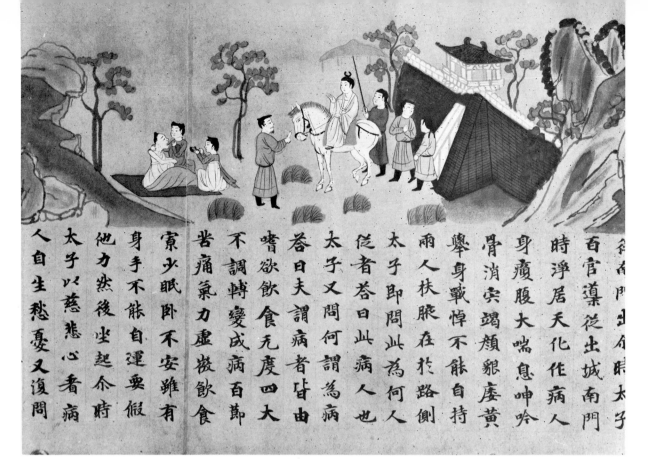

人自生愁憂又復問
太子以慈悲心看病
他力然後坐起介時
身手不能自運要假
寒少眠臥不安雖有
苦痛氣力虛羸飲食
嗜欲飲食无復四大
荅曰夫謂病者皆由
太子又問何謂為病
從者荅曰此病人也
太子即問此為何人
雨人扶腋在於路側
舉身戰悼不能自持
骨消宍竭顏貌黃
身癕腹大喘息呻吟
時淨居天化作病人
百官導從出城南門
爾南門出有時太子

text, are both considered to have had them at the time they were first produced.

Many different methods of combining the pictures and text are used. The first, used in the *E Inga-kyō* (Fig. 37), is to divide the scroll horizontally, with text below and pictures above. Another is to make the pictures continuous and write the text in special oblongs marked off on the upper part of the scroll, as in the *Kegon Gojūgo-sho Emaki* (Fig. 38). Both these methods came from China, and they were not followed up in Japan.

A third method is to alternate text and pictures, the picture following the appropriate piece of text. The number of pictures and pieces of text, thus, is in principle the same, and any discrepancy usually means that the work is imperfect, either text or pictures having been lost.

38   *Kegon Gojūgo-sho Emaki*

This form is perhaps the basic form of the Japanese picture scroll, the one adopted by the *Genji Monogatari Emaki* and a majority of other works. Besides this form there are, fourthly, a number of works, such as the *Fukutomi Zōshi* (Fig. 39) and the *Dōjō-ji Engi,* in which the text is scattered about amidst the pictures. In such cases, the basic narrative is usually omitted, the text consisting of the various characters' spoken words, placed near their pictures in the manner of many modern cartoons.

The third of the forms just mentioned has more varied uses than the rest, and as such is worth a closer look. In some cases, though the scroll has consistency and unity as a whole, each piece of text and its accompanying picture may have no direct connection, but only some quality in common with their predecessors on the scroll; the scroll, in other words, is a collection rather than the development of a theme. The *Yamai no Sōshi, Jigoku Zōshi,* and *Gaki Zōshi* are cases in point.

The *Yamai no Sōshi* is a one-scroll collection of accounts of strange deformities and diseases to be found in different parts of the country, while the *Jigoku Zōshi* and *Gaki Zōshi* are one-scroll collections of accounts of hell (*jigoku*) and "hungry demons" (*gaki*) taken from the

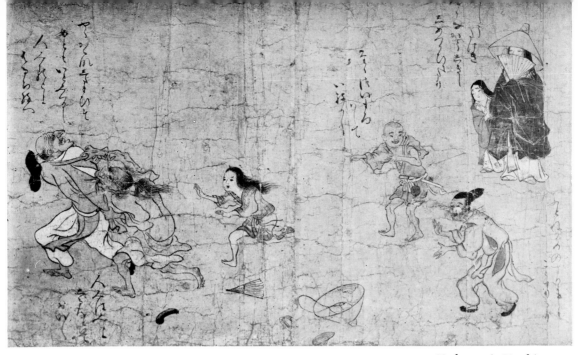

39  *Fukutomi Zōshi*

scriptures.  There is no "plot," and the pictures are mostly short, resembling illustrations.

Another use of the "alternating" method is in scrolls where the contents follow a continuous development and reach some more or less clear-cut conclusion at the end of the work.  There are two kinds again here.  One shows each story in a number of scenes resembling illustrations which alternate with the text, in the manner of the *Yamai no Sōshi*.  The other tells a whole story at one stretch in a continuous picture unbroken by text.

There is little to distinguish the scrolls such as the *Yamai no Sōshi* which are merely "collections" and those which, while "telling a story," chop it up into a number of non-continuous scenes.  As far as the composition of the scroll is concerned, they are of no particular interest.  The majority of scrolls fall into this category; the "continuous-picture" type of scroll, the composition of which requires considerably more ingenuity, is rarer, and scrolls of this type which—like the *Shigi-san Engi* and *Ban Dainagon Ekotoba*—are completely successful are rarer still.

The divisions just made do not mean, of course, that all scrolls

←

can be divided up into "collections" and scrolls that "tell a story." The *Ishiyama-dera Engi* and *Kasuga Gongen Reigen Ki,* for instance, each include a number of different tales of Buddhist and Shinto supernatural occurrences. The 48-scroll *Hōnen Shōnin Eden* and the 12-scroll *Ippen Shōnin Eden* are both collections of individual episodes from the lives of the two famous priests they deal with, but there is continuous development within each episode. Again, the *Shigi-san Engi* consists of three scrolls, each of them an independent, continuous work, yet the three have a common hero and combine to form an artistic whole.

Such scrolls thus represent a combination of the two types. Similarly, there are some scrolls which mingle the "continuous" picture and the independent, illustration-type picture.

Let us consider now some of the more noteworthy methods of composition peculiar to the picture scroll.

## 1) Relevance

A picture scroll is viewed by holding it in both hands, rolling with the right and unrolling with the left, and the eye travels from the right to the left of the picture. Perhaps the greatest pleasure, thus, is anticipation: what is going to appear next? The section of the scroll visible at any one moment is only about two feet out of a possible several dozen feet. When the scroll is divided up into a large number of separate pictures like illustrations, each can be viewed independently within the two feet or so available at any given moment. When the composition is continuous, however, the section visible is part of a whole in the development of which it must play an important part.

Each section in such a case is thus not interesting if it is com-

plete and independent in itself, even though it may be, formally, satisfactory. It must be a development of what is to follow. It must be given "relevance," in other words, and a large element of this relevance must be the inciting of curiosity as to what is to come. This device, a basic requirement in the composition of the *emaki,* can be seen at its most effective in the "Tobikura" scroll of the *Shigi-san Engi* (Pl. 1), the first scroll of the *Ban Dainagon Ekotoba* (Pl. 2), and the *Chōjū Giga* (Fig. 40).

## 2) Flow

Since everything in a picture scroll moves from right to left, a person moving from right to left is always "going," and a person moving from left to right is always "coming." And since by its nature the *emaki* picture begins on the right and develops towards the left, it is natural for the movement in its composition to be in the same direction. Since, in viewing the scroll, one's eye travels from right to left, everything moving in that direction creates a sense of flow, of smoothness, while everything moving in the opposite direction creates a sense of restlessness and shock.

With a scroll that offers some continuous narrative, the first section that we unroll with our right hand is, as it were, the prelude, while the main events lie still wrapped in mystery in our left hand. It is right and proper, therefore, that the main character should appear facing the left as we look at him, and should advance toward the left, our eye accompanying him as he goes.

Anyone who contradicts this natural convention of the *emaki* and travels from left to right moves toward the viewer and, crossing his field of vision, disappears to the right. He is going offstage, as it were, and will have no further part in the proceedings. The two scenes shown from the *Matsuzaki Tenjin Engi* and the *Kitano Tengin Engi* (Fig. 41 and 42) by Tosa Mitsunobu both show Son'i, the head of the Tendai sect of Buddhism, making his way across the flooded River Kamo on his way to court at the command of the Emperor Daigo. Yet though the subject is the same, the fact that the direction of the movements is different in the two cases creates quite a different effect.

Sometimes the same use of movement from left to right creates a type of shock by colliding, as it were, with the motion of the eye. A

42 *Kitano Tenjin Engi*

particularly good example is the picture of the boy sword-bearer in the "Engi Kaji" scroll of the *Shigi-san Engi* (Fig. 43). The fact that his progress as he rushes foward like the wind is contrary to the motion of the eye is extremely effective in heightening the effect of speed.

In short, any characters who appear moving against the flow give us the impression of being in some way extraordinary, or incidental to the main development, while those who move with the flow give a feeling of intimacy, of being "on our side."

## 3) Shifting Point of View

In a form such as the picture scroll where the composition is continuous, it is essential that variety be given, as the eye travels from

right to left, by varying the distance and angle from which things are viewed. The same things, thus, are seen sometimes close at hand, sometimes from afar; now from above, now from below. And with the shifting of the point of view, the viewer is invited sometimes to pictorial appreciation of a far-reaching scene, sometimes to a more dramatic consideration of one person or detail. This quality of three-dimensional movement, added to the movement from right to left, gives the *emaki* still another of its characteristic qualities.

One of the best examples of this quality is the "Amagimi" scroll of the *Shigi-san Engi*. The heroine Amagimi is traveling throughout the country in search of her younger brother, and the artist, in the freedom with which he follows her up hill and down dale, showing her

←——

now in close-up, now as a small part of a mighty perspective, creates a vivid illusion that we are actually accompanying her on her travels.

Another example is the scene in the *Kegon Engi* (Fig. 44), in which Zemmyo leaps into the sea in pursuit of the ship carrying away her lover, the priest Gishō. Though the scene as she leaps is shown from quite a distance, the dragon into which she is transformed is shown immediately in close-up, the sudden switch intensifying greatly the dramatic effect. A similar change from distance to close-up is seen in the *Matsu-zaki Tenjin Engi* (Fig. 45), where a distant scene looking down on the water gives way almost at once to a close-up on land, thus giving a great sense of immediacy to the human figures we encounter there.

This mobility of viewpoint is something which differentiates the picture scroll from the ordinary painting, with its static viewpoint. There is something in common with the modern movie, but whereas the latter shows only one scene at a time, the fact that the scroll is unrolled by hand means that two scenes painted from different viewpoints often unavoidably appear at once, creating a sense of unbalance or lack of proportion. This effect, however, sometimes gives the *emaki* a special charm that movies lack.

## 4) Perspective

Since the majority of Japanese picture scrolls tell some story or

relate historical events, the emphasis in the pictures tends to be on human beings, and on the main character or characters in particular. It is common, thus, to portray human beings larger than they should be in relation to their surroundings, and this in turn sometimes leads to effects of perspective unthinkable in Western pictures.

An example is shown from the Amagimi scroll of the *Shigi-san Engi* (Fig. 46). Amagimi, who is searching for the younger brother she has not met for 20 years, is seen with her attendant on the road to Nara. The two humans, in the center right of the picture, are shown proportionately larger than anything else. To the left of them are shown: above, the foot of a hill in close-up; in the center, a hill and a herd of deer in the mid-distance; and below, trees on a distant hill. This is just the reverse of the perspective familiar in the West, which places near objects at the bottom of the picture and sky or distant objects at the top. One could interpret it as an attempt to show the landscape from the point of view of the central figure, Amagimi. Viewed purely objectively, thus, the picture is odd in its effect, but if one first concentrates one's gaze on the central figures, bearing in mind their position and purpose, then views the landscape on the left from this standpoint, all sense of unnaturalness disappears.

The scene from the *Kitano Tenjin Engi* (Shōkyū version) (Fig. 47) shows Sugawara Michizane, who has been banished to a distant part of the country, on the summit of the Heaven-Worshipping Mountain, whither he has climbed to pray for redress of the wrongs done him. The Sugawara shown here is almost too large to get on the mountain on which he is standing, while below him are trees and deer far smaller than himself. The aim is obviously to focus attention on the tragic hero and his emotion as he appeals to heaven, and at the same time, by making the objects below him small, to emphasize the great height of the mountain.

This kind of perspective which emphasizes the main character and his emotions, subordinating the surrounding scene to a secondary, explanatory role, could perhaps be called a "perspective of ideas" as opposed to the "perspective of things" common in the West.

## 5) The Bird's-eye View

The "bird's-eye view" is not peculiar to the *emaki*, but is commonly used in Oriental art as a whole. Two factors, however, make it peculiarly suitable for the picture scroll: the fact that the scroll itself is always viewed from above, and the limitations imposed by the scroll's extreme narrowness

46  *Shigi-san Engi*

compared with its length, which make it difficult to show large stretches of nature or the movement of large numbers of people without some special device. It is easy thus to shift the point of vision in outdoor scenes, but difficult in indoor scenes.

This led the *emaki* artists to take the bold step of removing the roofs of the houses completely. The *Genji Monogatari Emaki* (Fig. 48), the *Makura no Sōshi Emaki* (Fig. 49), the *Monogatari Emaki* (Fig. 50), and the *Seikō-ji Engi* (Fig. 51) all use this device. Unrealistic though it is, it allows a view of several rooms at the same time, as well as conveying very vividly what is happening to the people in those rooms. The *Monogatari Emaki* goes so far as to remove a lintel that ought to be there in order to give a clearer view of the room. Again, in the scene shown from the *Seikō-ji Engi*, the roof of one room only is removed so as to show a divine being visiting the founder of the Seikō-ji Temple in his sleep.

The rules of perspective in the *emaki* almost never demand that parallel lines appear to converge with distance, or that human figures in the background be made smaller than those in the foreground. This was

almost certainly due not to any lack of knowledge of such rules, but to the difficulty of giving a sense of space and unity and allowing the human figures to move about freely within such a vertically narrow frame, and also to the emphasis on the human figures as opposed to their surroundings that we have already seen (Fig. 52).

## 6) Combined Points of View

We have already seen how the *emaki* achieves variety by altering the viewpoint freely from scene to scene. It is worth nothing here that

49   *Makura no Sōshi Emaki*

50 *Monogatari Emaki*

occasionally several different viewpoints are adopted in composing one scene. An example is the scene shown from the *Eshi no Sōshi* (Fig. 53), in which a side view is combined with a bird's-eye view. The scroll tells how a poor painter is informed that he has been made lord of the province of Iyo. At the height of his rejoicing, however, he finds that the land already belongs to someone else, and he and his family sink into ever more wretched circumstances.

The scene in question shows the painter's home, already fallen upon hard times. The messenger sent to survey the territory has just arrived back with the evil tidings. The artist emphasizes the distress of

51 *Seikō-ji Engi*

the painter and his wife by painting them large—almost exaggeratedly so—
and on a level with the eye. Within the same composition, however, we
are given a bird's-eye view of the derelict roof of their home as a witness
to their poverty.

This dual approach, in which the chief characters are shown in
close-up while their surroundings are given different treatment, is often
used in the *emaki,* and realistic proportion and perspective are often
sacrificed. The aim in such cases, however, is to show the main characters large and to subordinate their surroundings to an emphasizing or
explanatory role.

## 7) Slanting Lines

The use of slanting lines in the *emaki* in depicting roofs, verandas,
lintels, and the like is extremely common. This is a natural result of
the attempt to achieve the maximum degree of spatial depth in the use
of the bird's eye-view technique.

The natural slope of such lines in the picture scroll is down from
right to left, since this gives a sense of smooth motion to the eye as it

travels along the scroll from right to left.   This right-to-left slope, however, does not always convey a sense of smoothness and thus of stability.
A good example is the scene in the *Genji* scroll (Fig. 54) showing the
final parting of Genji and his mistress the Lady Murasaki.   Murasaki has
long been gravely ill, and autumn has found her wasted to a shadow.
One evening, as a wind blows, she has propped herself up to look out
at the garden, when Genji appears and addresses her affectionately.   They
spend their last hours together composing poems for each other, and the
next day at dawn the lady passes away.   In depicting the scene, the
artist has, it is true, made his lines slope down from right to left, but
he has given them an angle of between 45 and 50 degrees.   As a
result, the building tilts steeply, and the seated figures lack all sense of
stability.   This impression of instability heightens enormously the tragic
unease of the scene.

Lines sloping down from left to right, on the other hand, almost
always inhibit the sense of flow and deprive the picture of its stability.
A brilliant example of the use of such lines is the scene between Uji no
Nakagimi and Niō no Miya in the *Genji* scroll (Fig. 55).   Uji no

55  *Genji Monogatari Emaki*

Nakagimi is angry because Niō no Miya, her husband, has recently taken Yūgiri, the daughter of Minister of the Left, as an additional wife. At the same time the husband is suspicious of the relationship between his wife and Prince Kaoru, who is in love with her. The delicate interplay of emotions between them takes place on an autumn evening, and the flowering bush in the garden is swaying in the wind. The use of sloping lines is perfectly designed to create the requisite atmosphere of uncertainty and tragedy.

Where the actual content is concerned, the chief emphasis in the Japanese picture scroll is on personages and narrative. As we have already

53  *Eshi no Sōshi*

seen, the things depicted—even natural scenery and inanimate objects—all have some bearing on the characters in the narrative, whom they explain and on whom they comment, as it were, from the side. The two gateways shown in Figure 56 and Figure 57 both fulfill this same function, but they illustrate well two further uses of the sloping lines under discussion.

The first scene, from the *Ban Dainagon Ekotoba* (Fig. 56), shows the Kyoto townsfolk rushing in alarm through the Sujaku-mon Gate to see the Ōtemmon Gate on fire. The second, from the *Heiji Monogatari Emaki* (Fig. 57), shows the Emperor Nijō, who has been confined by the rebellious forces of Fujiwara Nobuyori and Minamoto no Yoshitomo, escaping in the guise of a court lady. Just as he emerges from the Sakuhei-mon Gate of the Imperial palace, his carriage is halted by the rebel guard.

Both gates have a close bearing on the human beings depicted, but the former, through which people are entering, is given a right-left slant, while the latter, from which the people have already emerged, has a left-right slant. This is an example of how, through the use of sloping lines, the inanimate objects shown are made to comment on the human beings not only spatially but, in a sense, temporally. The left-right slant has a carrying-forward quality, a quality of futurity, while the right-left slant has a quality of completion, of "pastness."

It would be ridiculous, of course, to try to formulate hard-and-fast rules on a subject such as this. There are examples which contradict what has been said here, these occasioned sometimes by the artist's desire for variety, sometimes merely by insensitive draftsmanship. The use of slanting lines remains, however, one of the most interesting technical devices to be found in the Japanese picture scroll.

## 8)  Repetition

Scrolls which are based on a continuous narrative necessarily involve the repeated appearance of one central figure or object at different points in time and space. The different ways in which this necessary repetition is handled form another interesting characteristic of the *emaki*.

(*a*)  The first case is where the same character appears again and again in scenes that are each spatially and temporally different from the rest. This is the most common method. One of the simplest examples is the *Jūni Innen emaki* (Fig. 58), where the hero, King Settaku, is shown subjugating twelve demons. Although the time and place is different for each

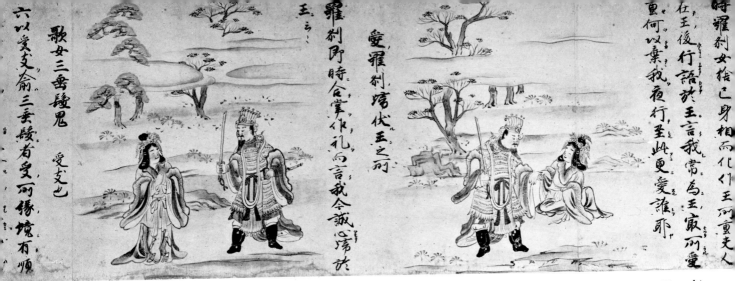

時羅刹女捨己身相而化作王而童走人
在王後行語於王言我常為王最而愛
重何以棄我夜行至此更愛誰耶

羅刹噂伏王之前
羅刹即時合掌作礼而言我今誠心端

愛

歌女三昧腰鬼　　受攴也
六以受攴偷三昧腰者受阿縁境有順

encounter, there is no sense of temporal progress from moment to moment; Settaku Ō is presented separately in each case, and the pictures themselves are divided up with no attempt at continuity.　Again, even in the *Genji* scroll, we are merely presented with a number of sections representing various stages in the career of the hero, and there is no development from moment to moment within each section.

Scrolls such as the *Sumiyoshi Monogatari Emaki* (Fig. 59) and the *Dōjō-ji Engi* (Fig. 60), on the other hand, set out to represent more realistically this transition through time.　In former, the hero is in love with a lady of high birth.　She has disappeared, however, and he seeks her high and low until finally he learns her whereabouts through the divine help of the Bodhisattva Kannon.　In the scene shown he has just arrived at Sumiyoshi, where the lady is in a nunnery.　On the extreme

←

right, the hero is seen asking the lady's serving woman to take him to her.  To the left in the same scene he is shown speaking to the abbess who has given her refuge, and the aged abbess is shedding tears.  Further to the left again, the serving woman is seen showing the hero to the lady's apartments, while at the upper extreme left he is sitting with her at last.  The technique here resembles that of the movie camera that follows the hero as he moves through time and space.

In the picture from the *Dōjō-ji Engi*, a young priest who has come to pay his respects at the Kumano Shrine is being chased by a woman with whom he has broken faith.  Here, instead of a single character, we have two, whose movements are noted from moment to moment, producing an effect still more complex and lively.

Both the *Sumiyoshi* and the *Dōjō-ji* scenes shown are more advanced

←—— 59  *Sumiyoshi Monogatari Emaki*

135

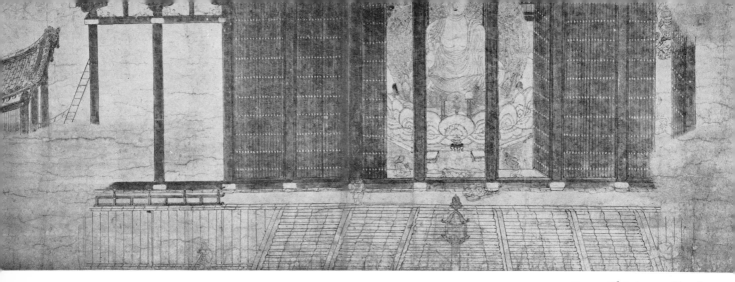

than their predecessors such as the *Jūni Innen Emaki* and the *Genji Monogatari Emaki* in so far as they come closer to employing the continuous-composition technique.   It is the first scroll of the *Shigi-san Engi,* however, that best succeeds in showing artistically the passage of time and sequence of events, working the same characters and objects a number of times into a continuous composition.

(*b*)   The second case is where the same character or characters make several appearances against the same background.   In some scrolls, such as the *Kibi Daijin Nittō Ekotoba*—which relates the adventures of the Japanese emissary Kibi no Makibi in T'ang China—the background itself is repeated several times without change, the human figures moving through time before it.   In others, however,—such as the *Shigi-san Engi* (Fig. 61), the *Ban Dainagon Ekotoba* (Fig. 62), the *Taima Mandara Engi* (Fig. 63),

63   *Taima Mandara Engi*

and the *Heiji Monogatari Emaki* (Fig. 64)—the background appears only once, and before it the same figure or figures appear several times to indicate the passage of time.

In the *Shigi-san Engi* picture the heroine Amagimi, who is searching for her younger brother, reaches the hall of the great Buddha at Nara and remains all night in supplication before the image. She dozes, and the Buddha, appearing to her in a dream, tells her her brother's whereabouts. Against one and the same background, we see her first (on the right) praying, then dozing before the image, then—in a posture that contrasts with and balances the first—offering thanks to the Buddha, and finally (on the extreme left) gazing out in the direction of Shigi-san, where her brother is.

64 *Heiji Monogatari Emaki*

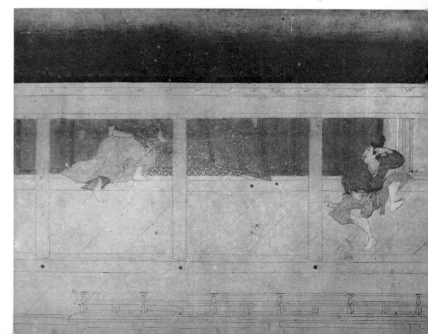

Figure 62 shows the scene from the *Ban Dainagon Ekotoba* where the sons of the Dainagon's treasurer and footman get into a fight. The treasurer rushes up and kicks the footman's son out of the way. At the top right, the two children are seen grappling with each other, with the treasurer running toward them from the left. Below this scene in the foreground the treasurer is seen kicking the other man's son, with his own son standing behind him. Then, at the top left, the treasurer's son is seen for a third time, being dragged away by his mother.

The scene from the *Taima Mandara Engi* (Fig. 63) shows, on the right, a manifestation of the Amida Buddha, who has appeared in response to a lady's prayers, showing her a representation of the Pure Land Paradise woven in lotus-fiber thread (the Taima Mandara in question). Then, in the foreground, the Buddha is seen bidding her farewell and finally, on the left, rising into the sky as the lady watches.

Both figures in Figure 64 are Fujiwara Nobuyori. One of the two chief plotters, along with Minamoto no Yoshitomo, of the Heiji rising, he has been keeping the Emperor confined in the palace. He has just been informed, however, that the Emperor has escaped and is rushing from place to place in consternation to confirm the report.

All the four examples just dealt with show two or three points in time in one picture that can be taken in at a glance. This method of composition was not originated by the *emaki,* having been used in the pictures on the stand of the *Tamamushi Zushi* miniature shrine in the

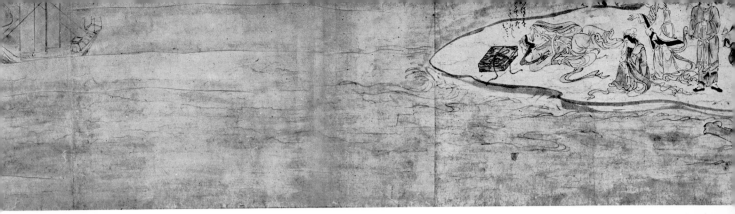

Hōryū-ji Temple.  It proved eminently suitable for the picture scroll, however, since it obviated wearisome repetition of the same background, and was also useful in suggesting, for example, a sense of haste or flurry in the human figures (as in the *Ban Dainagon* and *Heiji Monogatari* scrolls) or a sense of repose and stability in the background (as in the Great Buddha of the *Shigi-san Engi* scene).

(*c*)  In the third case, two events which occur simultaneously but in different places are shown in alternating pictures.  A good example is an episode from the biography of Gishō in the *Kegon Engi* (Fig. 65, Color Pl. 8).  Gishō, the founder of the Kegon sect in Korea, goes to T'ang China to study Buddhism.  There he meets a beautiful woman called Zemmyō, who falls in love with him.  Hearing that he is returning home, Zemmyō chases after him, only to find that his ship has already set sail.  She flings herself into the sea, is changed into a dragon, and carries the ship along on her back.  The scroll skilfully depicts the two simultaneous series of events—the ship setting out to sea and Zemmyo lamenting on the shore—in alternating pictures.

## 9)  Changes of Scene

The attempt to represent in pictures a story developing in time presents no problems if the scroll is content to be a collection of individual moments in time chosen from the story.  However, if the scroll links

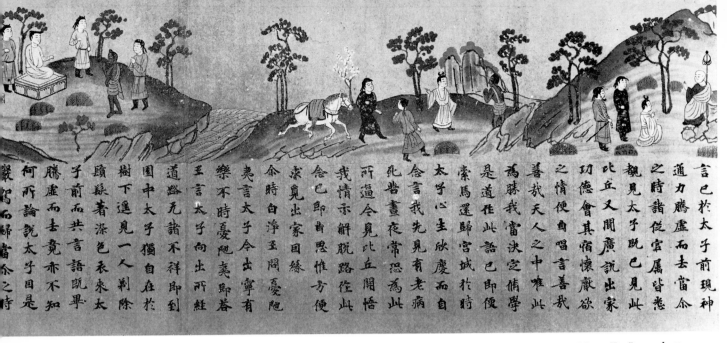

⟵    66   *E Inga-kyō*

together the scenes in a continuous composition the question arises of how to handle the links.

In the early *E Inga-kyō* (Fig. 66), natural objects such as mountains, rivers and trees are brought in to separate the scenes from each other. In this work, however, the device is a mere mechanical form and offers almost no variety whatsoever.

In the scene shown from the *Kitano Tenjin Engi* (Fig. 67), the right section shows the spirit of Sugawara Michizane, who has died at the Dazaifu, visiting the priest Son'i on Mount Hiei. He declares that he wishes to rid himself of the rancor he still harbors in death, and asks Son'i not to use the power of the law to hinder him. Son'i replies that he has no alternative but to comply with an official order. Michizane, therefore, spits out onto the door a pomegranate that Son'i has given him, whereupon it becomes a flame and burns; this is the scene that is shown on the left. The two scenes are separated by a stream in this case.

A river is used for a similar purpose in the scene from the *Ippen Shōnin Eden* (Fig. 68). The wife of the son of the priest of Kibitsu Shrine is converted to Buddhism by Saint Ippen during her husband's

← 67 *Kitano Tenjin Engi*

absence, and lets Ippen shave her head. The returning husband is enraged to find his wife become a nun and chases after Ippen, who is shown in the right-hand scene confronting the husband as he rushes at him with drawn sword. The left-hand scene shows the husband himself having his head shaved, having ended up by being converted in his turn.

*Kasuga Gongen Reigen Ki* (Fig. 69) contains a scene in which a deity of the Kasuga Shrine inspires a woman of the Tachibana family to give a divine message dissuading Meikei Shōnin of Toga-no-o from going abroad. The woman, who abstained from food and devoted herself to prayer and sutra-reading after the visitation of the Kasuga deity, is shown seated to the right reading a sutra. The same woman appears on the ceiling in the next room. She is swollen with child, but she has easily climbed to the ceiling and is here delivering the divine message of the deity. Listening to her with clasped hands is Meikei Shōnin, with others seated behind him. Sliding doors are used to separate these two adjacent scenes, which occur in two rooms of the same house.

The first scene from the *Eshi no Sōshi* (Fig. 70) shows the poor painting master who has been made lord of Iyo telling his family the

→ 68 Ippen Shōnin Eden

good news. He invites his relatives in to celebrate, and the second scene shows a drinking party in progress (see page 85). The two scenes are set in two rooms of the same house, and a wooden partition serves to separate them from each other.

The different scenes in the last three examples, though separated one from the other, are very close and can be taken in at one glance. In this they are similar to the examples dealt with on earlier pages, but in this case the backgrounds are different, so that strictly speaking the treatment is not the same. Even so, the close juxtaposition of the different scenes does enhance the dramatic effect—the suddenness of the fire-spitting, the swiftness with which Ippen turns the tables, the rapidity with which the painter's family starts celebrating.

Let us look at two further, slightly more advanced, examples of this technique.   The scene from the *Ippen Shōnin Eden* (Fig. 71) shows the one preceding that shown on page 142.   On the right, the wife is having her head shaved, while on the left she stands gazing out of the house, already in the garb of a nun.   Figure 72 is from the *Bakemono Zōshi,* a collection of ghost stories.   As a woman is saying her invocations to Amida Buddha one night, a strange monk with pointed ears keeps peeping out at her from behind a closet.   When she investigates in the morning, she finds that the monk was really a rotten, broken wine bottle.   On the right, the monk is seen peeping in at the woman saying her prayers.   On the left, the woman is relating the night's happenings.

In both these cases, both the scenes are set in rooms, but the rooms are not set side by side as in the *Eshi no Sōshi*. Instead, interest is added by changing the angle. The effect is rather like the "half-turn" of the revolving stage used in the Japanese Kabuki, which reveals to the audience both new scenery and new aspects of scenery already familiar.

Technically ingenious though these methods are, the scene-changing device most skilfully used in the Japanese picture scroll is undoubtedly the use of mist and empty space. The joint between two successive scenes is

←

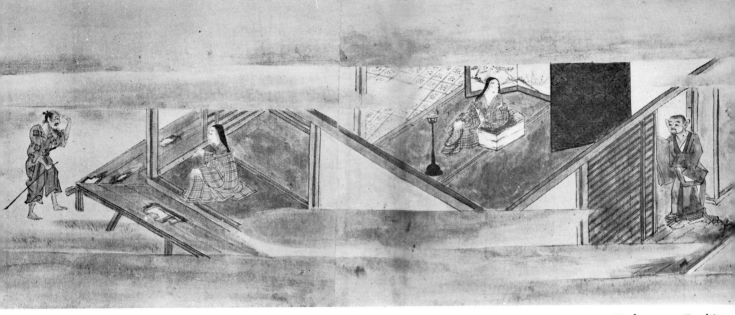

sometimes softened and blurred as though covered by a mist or haze; or sometimes the ends of the two scenes are "faded out," leaving an empty space in between. The best example extant is the *Shigi-san Engi* (Fig. 73), particularly the "Tobikura" scroll. The example shown here is the appearance of the boy sword-bearer in the second scroll of the work, where the roof on the left is "faded out" before it reaches the edge of the paper so as to make smoother the transition to the next scene.

The section of the *Heiji Monogatari Emaki* (Fig. 74) shown includes two scenes: on the right, Fujiwara Nobuyori is being told, to

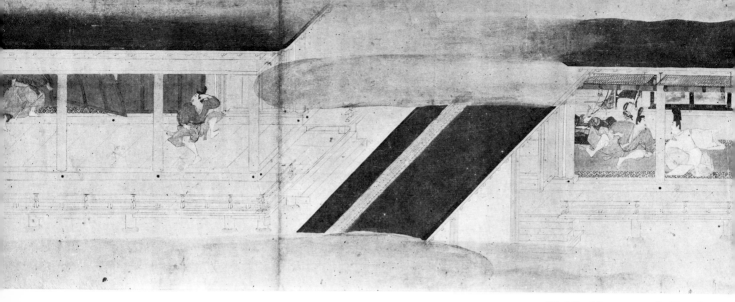

←—— 74 *Heiji Monogatari Emaki*

his great consternation, that the Empereor, whom he was holding in confinement, has escaped; while on the left he is shown rushing from room to room to confirm the escape for himself. The two scenes are divided by a roof, obscured at the top and the bottom by banks of mist, which smooth the transition and at the same time effectively suggest the time: dawn.

This method of changing the scene is interesting as a precursor of the cinematic "fadeout"; it is also typical of the delicacy with which the Japanese artist always strives to introduce at least a touch of nature into any portrayal of the fortunes of human beings.

# Style

WE have seen earlier how paintings of Buddhist subjects came to Japan along with the many other cultural elements from the continent that flowed in with the introduction of Buddhism, and how it was followed thereafter by a succession of different styles of painting from the continent.

The first style of painting, introduced along with Buddhism, was that of Six Dynasties China (around the middle of the sixth century A.D.). Next, from the early part of the Nara period (middle of the seventh century), the T'ang style was introduced and dominated painting in Japan until the beginning of the Heian period (ninth century). The paintings of this period were mostly produced by naturalized painters from the continent, or by members of the schools they founded.

However, in the latter part of the Heian period, in the tenth century, there at last arose a new native culture freed of the shackles of T'ang civilization, and with it was born the *yamato-e,* the first type of painting that, painted by Japanese, was Japanese in both content and style.

The picture scroll, which was born at the same time as this first flowering of native culture, grew up on the foundation provided by this *yamato-e* style, and shared its fate throughout the centuries, finally declining with it in the Muromachi period (sixteenth century). The inseparable connection between the two is witnessed by the fact that the picture scroll is sometimes known as *yamato-e emaki.* One cannot ignore the *yamato-e* style and give the name *emaki* to everything produced in Japan in the form of a scroll with pictures. For instance, Sesshū's Long Landscape Scroll (*Sansui Chōkan*), Hishikawa Moronobu's Scrolls of Manners and Customs (*Fūzoku Gakan*), and Maruyama Ōkyo's Seven Tribulations and Seven Happinesses (*Shichinan Shichifuku Zukan*) are all, in form, painted scrolls, but their style is not that of the *yamato-e* and they cannot, thus, be considered within the province of the *emaki.*

The term *yamato-e* does not, however, indicate one simple, uniform style. In the course of the picture scroll's development, the subject matter became very varied, and as the content became richer the *yamato-e* style used to express it also became more diverse and complex in its techniques.

*Yamato-e* picture scrolls can be divided, broadly, into those that use color and those that do not.

Scrolls in color can be further subdivided into three categories: those in which use of color is the main element; those in which the emphasis is on line; and those in which equal importance is attached to both color and line.

The most typical example of the primary dependence on color is, of course, the *Genji Monogatari Emaki* (Fig. 75, Color Pl. 2). The style is that known as *tsukuri-e,* in which a sketch is first made, then covered

←—— 75 *Genji Monogatari Emaki*

over thickly with paint, the forms being altered freely with successive layers of paint until the picture is finished. The technique here resembles that of modern oil-painting, and the paints themselves are opaque. Finally, the forms are given clear shape and the boundaries between color and color defined by *kakiokoshi,* or "touching up"— a *yamato-e* technique in which the outlines are retraced in India ink after the rest of the paint has been applied. These lines, however, are always kept fine, soft, unexpressive, and unobtrusive. They are only required to delineate: it is the color—its distribution, balance, and rhythms—that organizes the picture. Never is the line allowed to express anything positive such as speed, movement, or mass; instead, rich yet refined colors portray a peaceful world of sensuousness and sentiment. If one looks at the *Genji* scroll as it is today, one notices quite coarse black lines—in the clothing worn by the figures, for instance. This however, is because the color has flaked off badly, revealing the preliminary sketch underneath, which was originally, of course, completely painted over in thick colors.

Other examples of the *tsukuri-e* technique besides the *Genji* scroll are the *Nezame Monogatari Emaki* and *Murasaki Shikibu Nikki Emaki.* All

76  *Genji Monogatari Emaki* (Detail)

*Genji Monogatari Emaki* (Detail)

these works portray the lives of the court nobles of the Heian period, and their literary themes are the esthetic and emotional lives of these nobles. The aim of the painters of the scrolls, thus, was not so much to illustrate a narrative as to bring out as vividly as possible the exquisite moods of the original work. The scrolls being based on courtly literature of the Heian age, their prime aim, it would seem, became to reproduce the same romantic spirit that pervaded that literature. For this, the *tsukuri-e* technique was ideal; in portraying the men and women murmuring to each other behind the hanging screens in the inner apartments of the palace, what could be more suited than this style that filled the whole surface with elegant color imbued with an undefinable melancholy, and eschewed any lines that might suggest movement?

The facial expressions, similarly, are without exception placid, almost as though their owners were asleep. On the plump, inverted-pear-shaped faces the eyes are single, narrow, near-horizontal lines, the noses tiny hooks (Fig. 76). All are stereotypes almost entirely devoid of individuality: without the text, in fact, one would have difficulty in identifying the characters represented.

Yet this very deletion of any specific expression, this denial to the face of any personality, acts in the same way as the Noh mask, which, by compressing inward all human emotions, manages to exude an even stronger generalized mood. All the faces here are wrapped in a profound stillness, seemingly lost in an eternity where there is sentiment but no time.

The oldest appearance of the word *tsukuri-e* is in the *Tales of Genji*, where the word is already used in the sense of "colored picture" as opposed to the *sumi-e* or India ink picture. The *Sankai Ki* reports that the official

77 *Shigi-san Engi* (Detail)

bureau of painting in the year 1184—at the end of the Heian period—
was made up of three departments responsible for producing *sumigaki*
(India ink pictures), lightly-colored pictures, and *tsukuri-e* respectively. This
division of labor, incidentally, was typical of the day: the first picture in
the *Suzumushi* section of the *Genji Monogatari Emaki,* for instance, has
flaked badly, and between the lines of the preliminary India ink sketch thus
revealed beneath can be seen the detailed instructions written in for those
who were to apply the pigments.

Where line in the type of *emaki* just dealt with is inexpressive,
rich colors being relied on to create a world of quiet sentiment, there is
another type in which the greatest emphasis is placed on the strokes of
the brush. Speed and variety of line combine to create a world of
movement where the aim is no longer to suggest to the emotions, but to
recount to the mind. The most typical example is the *Shigi-san Engi.*

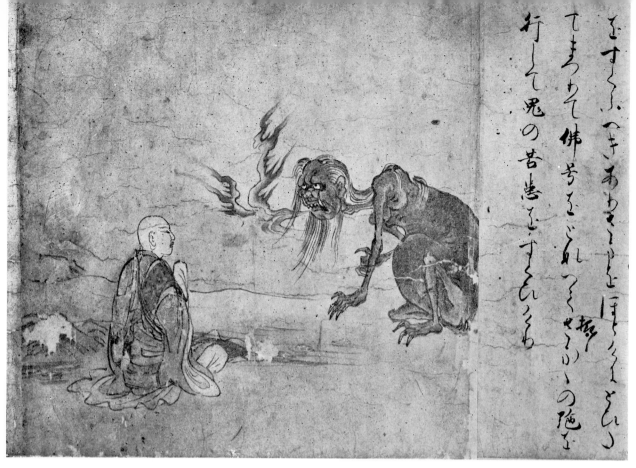

78　*Gaki Zōshi*

In the *Shigi-san Engi* (Fig. 77, Color Pl. 3), color is relegated to a secondary role throughout. In some places the coloring is fairly rich, but even here it remains subordinate and complementary to the movement of the line. Line here is not, as in the *Genji* scroll, devoid of variety and drawn with a rigid brush, but rich in lightness, speed, and freedom. The human figures thus depicted are stimulated by the animation of the line into perpetual activity, and the picture, through the vivacity of its lines, creates in the viewer a sense of vivid movement. The flowing, restless nature of the line inevitably means that the picture suggests the passage of time and lends itself to narrative. Again, whereas in the *Genji* scroll the whole surface is covered with paint, which shuts in the objects depicted, and restricts their activities, here the background is left free for them to move about in as they wish.

Differing thus from *Genji* in style, it is natural that the *Shigi-san*

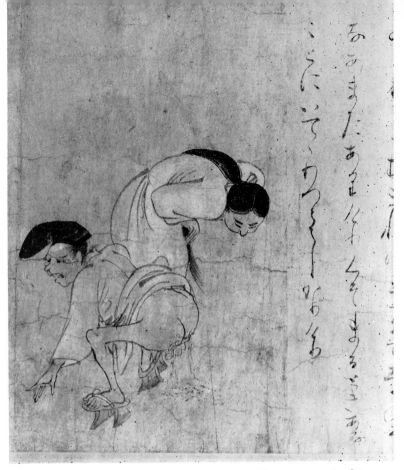

79　*Yamai no Sōshi*

*Engi* should differ from it in its subject matter also. Where *Genji* is passive and atmospheric, the *Shigi-san Engi* is active and dramatic. Where *Genji* is lyrical, *Shigi-san Engi* is epic and descriptive. Where *Genji* deals in interiors and the aristocratic world, the action of *Shigi-san Engi* more often takes place outdoors and depicts the life of the common people. Finally, while the faces of the characters in *Genji* are stereotyped and lack individuality, the *Shigi-san Engi* emphasizes, sometimes even exaggerates, individual expressions.

The style and aims of the two types, thus, are utterly different; where one uses color to express the mood evoked by the theme, the other relies on line to narrate a story. The contrast between the two, moreover, is so marked that neither could ever possibly be considered as having developed from the other.

Other works, beside the *Shigi-san Engi,* which belong to this category

81  *Kitano Tenjin Engi*

are the *Kokawa-dera Engi,* the *Jigoku Zōshi* (Color Pl. 6), the *Gaki Zōshi* (Fig. 78, Color Pl. 7), and the *Yamaino Sōshi* (Fig. 79).

There is one masterpiece that in its style stands just midway between the two types represented by the *Genji Monogatari Emaki* and the *Shigi-san Engi* respectively. It is the *Ban Dainagon Ekotoba* (Fig. 80, Color Pl. 4). In the rich variety and rhythms of its free, flowing India ink lines, it is an excellent example of the *Shigi-san Engi* type of scroll, while at the same time the comparatively richly-colored *tsukuri-e* style used in some places in the scroll puts it in the same category as the *Genji* scroll.

80  *Ban Dainagon Ekotoba*

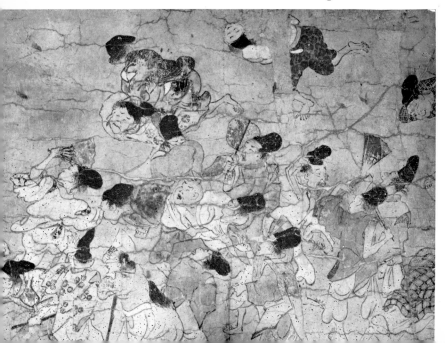

82 *Ise Shin-Meisho Uta-awase Emaki*

It represents, in fact, an exceedingly skilful compromise between the two styles. Its subject matter is a very eventful episode in Japan's history; large numbers of different characters make their appearance, from the Emperor, court nobles, and samurai down to the common people at the lowest levels of society, and every technical device is used in portraying these varied classes of people.

At the end of the Heian period, the two styles represented by the *Genji* and *Shigi-san* scrolls existed side by side and distinct from each other, but in the Kamakura period the distinction gradually disappeared, and a compromise style became increasingly popular. Color and line failed equally to dominate the field. It is true that, encouraged by the subsequent introduction of Sung styles of painting, with their emphasis on line, the importance attached to line increased, but no further works appeared which relied on it completely as the *Shigi-san Engi* had done.

In accordance with the increasing diversity of the *emaki's* subject matter, the compromise style just mentioned showed itself in a variety of

83   *Heiji Monogatari Emaki* (Detail)

forms.   For example, the Shōkyū version of the *Kitano Tenjin Engi* (Fig.
81, Color Pl. 9) is painted in a heavy-handed style employing strong
lines and rich colors.   The *Saigyō Monogatari Emaki* and *Ise Shin-Meisho
Uta-awase Emaki* (Fig. 82), on the other hand, employ a more refined
style with delicate lines and light colors.   There are others, again, such as
the *Sanjūroku Kasen Emaki* (Color Pl. 10), formerly in the possession of the
Satake family, where line and color alike are delicate yet sumptuous.   There
are also scrolls where the style is varied to suit the subject within one and
the same work, using color to evoke mood and line to depict action; rich
colors in showing the lives of the nobility, black lines with little color
for the common people.   In the *Heiji Monogatari Emaki* (Fig. 83, Color
Pl. 11), the clothing of some characters is painted in extremely rich colors
while those same characters' arms and legs are done in lively lines and
pale colors.   There are also cases where both rich and delicate coloring

are used in the same section of the picture.   In this way, the *emaki* carried the development of the *yamato-e* further by exploring the many and varied possibilities of a compromise between line and color.

All the scrolls discussed so far have employed color; it remains to discuss works in the *hakubyō* style.   The term *hakubyō* usually refers to pictures relying entirely on black, India ink lines, though it also covers pictures employing a little faint color as well.   Typical examples are the *Chōjū Giga* (Fig. 84), the *Makura no Sōshi Emaki* (Fig. 85), and the *Zuishin Teiki Emaki* (Fig. 86).   These three scrolls, however, all present individual characteristics of their own.

In the *Chōjū Giga* skilful use is made of the distinction between thick and thin India ink; the lines are broad, light in touch, and full of variety and speed.   The speed, moreover, has fluency and the variety has flexibility.   The whole effect, thus, is fresh and unpretentious, without the slightest awkwardness.   Nor does the line serve merely to demarcate; instead, it plays a more constructive role in forming the picture, which is at once dynamic and descriptive.   So light and fluent is the line that the monkeys, hares, and frogs it depicts seem to leap and sport with complete freedom as if they were alive.

85 *Makura no Sōshi Emaki* (Detail)

The *Makura no Sōshi Emaki,* on the other hand, is composed of extremely delicate outlines and India ink surfaces of varying degrees of intensity. Hair and details of the furnishings, for instance, are done in uniform black, while the eyebrows are shaded and the lips are just touched with red, which is the only color used. Unlike the lines in the *Chōjū*

86  *Zuishin Teiki Emaki*

*Giga,* the outlines here serve merely to border space, yet the arrangement and combination of the delicate threads of line, combined with the interplay of black and white as the white background of the paper gives way first to light wash and then to black, create an effect of richness and evoke fa mood o quiet elegance. In a manner, it achieves through the disposition of black and white the same effect as the *Genji Monogatari Emaki* does with the *tsukuri-e* technique. In fact, a comparison between the quietist, evocative *Makura no Sōshi Emaki* and the active, descriptive *Chōjū Giga* calls to mind a similar comparison between two opposing types in the colored scroll—the *Genji Monogatari Emaki* and the *Shigi-san Engi*.

The *Zuishin Teiki Emaki* is done in uniformly fine lines with no variations in thickness, but they have the same lightness, verve, and speed as the lines in the *Chōjū Giga*. True, there is not the sense of variety with flexibility that one derives from the *Chōjū Giga,* yet the pictures have the same carefree, light touch as a sketch, and the faces of the humans shown have true individuality. It differs from other *hakubyo* works such as the *Chōjū Giga* and *Makura no Sōshi Emaki* in being touched lightly with color on the faces and the horses' tassels. The *Kuge Retsuei Zukan* is another scroll in the same category.

# Subject Matter

THE Chinese picture scroll, under the influence of which the Japanese *emaki* came into being and developed, had from early times dealt with a wide range of subjects—history, ancient customs, portraits, landscapes, still life, etc. The Japanese *emaki* too may, for all we know, have dealt with similar subjects at first. However, it was in the presentation of narratives that it achieved its greatest development. The Chinese scrolls had also included this type in the early days, but in later times (particularly from Sung onward) the most popular subjects were landscapes and still life, while little progress was made in the depiction of human relationships and social conditions.

The *emaki,* on the other hand, though occasionally recording manners and customs or portraying famous personages, deals chiefly with human relationships, and covers, moreover, a wide range—the tragic and the comic, wars and love affairs, the sublime and the ridiculous, grief and rejoicing. Again, though the artists of the *emaki* were not necessarily indifferent to landscapes—the *Shigi-san Engi, Saigyō Monogatari Emaki,* and

*Ippen Shōnin Eden* all show favorite scenic spots—their landscapes are not independent scenes as are the Chinese, but almost always appear in relation to the main character, who is usually traveling through them or sightseeing. It is a characteristic of the Japanese picture scroll, thus, that it never strays far from human stories and human affairs. In this respect, it is a typical manifestation of the national love of a good tale.

Generally speaking, Japanese picture scrolls can be divided into two main categories: religious scrolls, usually made for some didactic purpose, and non-didactic scrolls, the aim of which is purely to entertain.

The majority of religious scrolls deal with Buddhist themes, but there are also some Shintō works. Their subject matter is taken chiefly from the Buddhist scriptures, the annals of shrines or temples, and the lives of celebrated clerics. Those based on the scriptures are illustrations of sutras, expositions of the sutras, or sermons, and extant examples include the *E Inga-kyō,* the *Kegon Gojūgo-sho Emaki,* the *Jūni Innen Emaki,* the *Jigoku Zōshi,* and the *Gaki Zōshi.* The second type of religious scroll relates the circumstances of the founding of a particular Buddhist temple or shrine, or divine occurrences connected with the deity enshrined there. There are many such works, typical examples being the *Shigi-san Engi,* the *Kokawa-dera Engi,* the *Taima Mandara Engi,* the *Ishiyama-dera Engi,* the *Dōjō-ji Engi,* the *Kitano Tenjin Engi,* the *Kasuga Gongen Reigen Ki,* and the *Sannō Reigen Ki.* The third type relates the achievements of celebrated priests of the past and extols their virtures. The *Kegon Engi,* the *Kōbō Daishi Eden,* the *Hōnen Shōnin Eden,* the *Ippen Shōnin Eden,* and many other scrolls belong to this category.

The scrolls intended primarily to entertain are usually literary, narrative, and secular in content. One of the most important sources of subject matter is the classical romances of the Heian period, or the neo-classical literature of the Kamakura period. Set against the life of the court nobles of Heian times, their chief characteristic is their refinement of feeling. The most famous specimen extant is the *Genji Monogatari Emaki;* others are the *Nezame Monogatari Emaki,* the *Murasaki Shikibu Nikki Emaki,* the *Makura no Sōshi Emaki,* and the *Sumiyoshi Monogatari Emaki.*

Another type is based on odd events, strange tales, and satirical accounts of actual life, and relies as a whole on the intrinsic interest of what they have to relate. They include the *Ban Dainagon Ekotoba,* the *Shōgun-zuka Emaki,* the *Yamai no Sōshi,* the *Eshi no Sōshi,* the *Haseo-kyō Zōshi,* the *Koshibagaki Zōshi,* and the *Chigo Zōshi.*

The *otogi-zōshi* scrolls are a group of works based on the popular tales of the same name of the Muromachi period. Though they cover a wide range of subjects, they are naive and have little literary value. Typical examples are the *Fukutomi Zōshi,* the *Tsuchigumo Zōshi,* the *Bakemono Zōshi,* the *Ōeyama Ekotoba,* and the *Zegaibō Ekotoba.*

Another set of scrolls deals with celebrated historical battles and the exploits of the samurai who took part in them. Records show that the number of such scrolls produced was far from small, but the only ones extant today are *Heiji Monogatari Emaki,* the *Mōko Shūrai Ekotoba,* the *Zen-kunen Kassen Emaki,* the *Go-sannen Kassen Emaki,* and the *Yūki Kassen Ekotoba.*

The scrolls based on *waka* poetry are collections of portraits of poets or of landscapes mentioned in the poems; they include some works which place pictures of the "Sages of Poetry" or other celebrated poets alongside their poems, while others illustrate "poetry tournaments" (*uta-awase*), setting pictures of the competing poets or of landscapes to the right and left of the poems. Such works, of course, are entirely lacking in the narrative element. Extant works of this kind are the Satake version of the *Sanjūroku Kasen Emaki,* the *Tōhoku-in Shokunin Uta-awase Emaki,* and the *Ise Shin-Meisho Uta-awase Emaki.*

Finally, there are the "documentary" *emaki,* which are collections of portraits or pictures of events with some historical significance, and include also works dealing with cows, horses, and so on. Surviving specimens include the *Kuge Retsuei Zukan,* the *Tennō Sekkan Daijin Ei,* the *Chūden Gyokai Zukan,* the *Zuishin Teiki Emaki,* and the *Bai Sōshi.*

# Explanation of the Thirty Principal *Emaki*

(chronological order)

1 *E Inga-kyō*

2 *Genji Monogatari Emaki*

3 *Shigi-san Engi*

4 *Ban Dainagon Ekotoba*

5 *Chōjū Giga*

6 *Nezame Monogatari Emaki*

7 *Jigoku Zōshi*

8 *Gaki Zōshi*

9 *Yamai no Sōshi*

10 *Kokawa-dera Engi*

11 *Kegon Engi*

12 *Kibi Daijin Nitto Ekotoba*

13 *Taima Mandara Engi*

14 *Kitano Tenjin Engi*

15 *Sanjūroku Kasen Emaki*

16 *Murasaki Shikibu Nikki Emaki*

17 *Heiji Monogatari Emaki*

18 *Zuishin Teiki Emaki*

19 *Saigyō Monogatari Emaki*

20 *Mōko Shūrai Ekotoba*

21 *Tōsei Eden*

22 *Ippen Shōnin Eden*

23 *Ishiyama-dera Engi*

24 *Kasuga Gongen Reigen Ki*

25 *Hōnen Shōnin Eden*

26 *Eshi no Sōshi*

27 *Komakurabe Gyōkō Emaki*

28 *Makura no Sōshi Emaki*

29 *Fukutomi Zōshi Emaki*

30 *Dōjō-ji Engi*

# 1 E Inga-kyō
## (The Sutra of Cause and Effect)

Artist unknown.
Nara period (8th century).
Color on paper.
Height 26.36 cm.
One scroll in the Jōbonrendai-ji, Kyoto.
One scroll in the Hōon-in, Kyoto.
One scroll in the Tokyo University of Arts.
National Treasure.


This is an illustrated version of "The Sutra of Cause and Effect in Past and Present," describing the *Honjōdan* (previous existence) and the *Butsuden* (historical life) of the Buddha. The sutra is transcribed along the lower part of the scroll, and the illustrations explaining the text run along above it. The sutra is written in the severe "block" characters of T'ang China, but the illustrations imitate the painting style of the Six Dynasties period in China and show an extremely unsophisticated artistry. This is a Japanese copy of a form which came from China. The painter is unknown, but it was probably executed by a professional painter of the period.

## 2 Genji Monogatari Emaki
## (The Tales of Genji)

Attributed to Fujiwara Takayoshi.
Late Heian period.
Color on paper.
Originally four scrolls.
Three scrolls in the Reimei-kai, Tokyo.
One scroll in the Gotō Art Museum, Tokyo.
National Treasure.

These scrolls are based on "The Tales of Genji" (written by Murasaki Shikibu in the 11th century), a romantic novel depicting the life of the nobility in the Heian period with Prince Genji as its hero. Crucial scenes are selected from the story for illustration. Originally, there were probably a large number of scrolls, but at present only three remain. For better preservation, the sections of painting and text are kept separately in boxes. There are twenty sections of text and nineteen sections of painting, corresponding to *Yomogyū, Sekiya, Kashiwagi, Yokobue, Suzumushi, Yūgiri, Minori, Takekawa, Hashihime, Sawarabi, Yadorigi,* and *Azumaya* from the fifty-four chapters of "The Tales of Genji."

In painting each scene, a line drawing was first made, then painted over with bright pigments, and finally the lines were delicately redrawn in black ink to create an effect of refined beauty. An abbreviated painting technique called *hikime-kagihana* (literally, line-eye hook-nose) is used. Although this deprives the figures of individual facial expressions, the mood of the story is well captured. An extremely flowing style of calligraphy combines with the painting to enhance the atmosphere of elegance.

Tradition attributes this work to the famous court painter Fujiwara Takayoshi (12th century), but examination of the style clearly shows it was painted by several artists. Together with *Shigi-san Engi, Ban Dainagon Ekotoba,* and *Chōjū Giga,* it must be numbered among the surviving scroll masterpieces.

# 3 *Shigi-san Engi*
## (The Legends of Shigi-san Temple)

Attributed to Kakuyū (Toba Sōjō).
Late Heian period (12th century).
Color on paper.
Three scrolls.
Height 31.5 2cm.
In the Chōgosonshi-ji, Nara.
National Treasure.

This is the story of the Buddhist prelate Myōren, who, in the early 10th century, made the Chōgoson Temple on Mount Shigi in Nara Prefecture famous. It is mainly concerned with the miracles he performed.

The first scroll relates the story of the magic flying bowl of Myōren, who secluded himself on Mount Shigi. The wonderful iron bowl carries the rice storehouse of a wealthy man from the foot of the mountain to the top, and Myōren, at the request of the wealthy man, has the magic bowl fly the rice bales back to his house. In the second scroll, Myōren is requested to pray for the recovery from illness of Emperor Daigo. The Emperor is restored to health through the power of the Buddha without Myōren's stirring from Mount Shigi. The third scroll depicts the story of a Buddhist nun, the elder sister of Myōren, who remained in their native district of Shinano. The nun goes up to Nara to visit her younger brother, and in a dream she is told by the *Daibutsu* (Great Buddha) of the Tōdai-ji to go to Mount Shigi, where she finally meets him.

This work employs the flowing lines characteristic of the *yamato-e,* and the expressions and movements of the characters are conveyed with great liveliness. The work also shows a great fluidity of composition, conveying with consummate skill the development of the story in time. According to tradition, the painter of these scrolls was the famous Kakuyū (1053-1140, known generally by the familiar name of Toba Sōjō), a high Buddhist prelate of the Heian period who was also an artistic genius.

## 4 *Ban Dainagon Ekotoba*
## (The Story of the Courtier Ban Dainagon)

Attributed to Tokiwa Mitsunaga.
Late Heian period (12th century).
Color on paper.
Three scrolls.
Height 31.52 cm.
In the collection of Sakai Tadahiro, Tokyo.
National Treasure.

This scroll depicts an incident during the reign of Emperor Seiwa (9th century) in which Dainagon Tomo (Ban) no Yoshio, in order to ensnare a political foe, Minamoto no Makoto, Minister of the Left, sets fire to Ōtemmon (Ōten Gate) in front of the palace and claims that it is the minister's doing. However, the true facts are exposed and Dainagon is exiled.

This work employs a continuous style of composition, unfolding the story with a skill typical of the *emaki* at its best. The technique of line and coloring and the energetic depiction of human faces and movements are also extremely skilful. This work is, in fact, one of the best among existing picture scrolls. The painter was probably Tokiwa Mitsunaga, a famous artist of the late Heian period (12th century).

## 5 Chōjū Giga
## (The Cartoons of Animals)

Attributed to Kakuyū (Toba Sōjō).
Heian and Kamakura periods (12th and 13th centuries).
Ink on paper.
Four scrolls.
Height 30.61 and 31.81.
Owned by Kōzan-ji, Kyoto.
National Treasure.

These are generally called "The Frolicking Animal Scrolls," but the contents of each scroll are different. The first scroll portrays monkeys, rabbits, frogs, etc., which seem to be playfully impersonating human beings. The second scroll pictures horses, cows, hawks, eagles, lions, tigers, dragons, etc. in their natural forms; real and imaginary animals are intermingled. The third scroll is divided into two parts, with Buddhist priests and laymen enjoying games of chance in the first part, and with monkeys, rabbits, and frogs sporting in imitation of human beings in the second part. The fourth scroll, similar to the first half of the third scroll, shows Buddhist priests and laymen at play.

All the scrolls are line drawings in India ink. The first and second scrolls are by the same painter, but the first and the second parts of the third scroll and the fourth scroll each appear to be by different painters. Among the four scrolls, the first is the best, and is the finest masterpiece of line drawing to be produced in Japan. The first and second scrolls appear to be works of the Heian period (12th century), while the third and fourth scrolls are probably from the Kamakura period (13th century). Tradition attributes the work to Kakuyū (Toba Sōjō), the famous priest-painter of the Heian period, but this is not certain.

## 6 Nezame Monogatari Emaki
(The "Nezame Monogatari")

Artist unknown.
Late Heian period (12th century).
Color on paper.
One scroll.
Height 25.76 cm.
In the Yamato Bunka-kan Collection, Nara.
National Treasure.

The basis of this scroll is the "Nezame Monogatari," a literary work of the late Heian period. The original number of scrolls is unknown, but only one survives today. The text is jumbled, and it is difficult to

understand the plot. The work is painted in the thick-pigmented *tsukuri-e* technique and tends strongly toward the decorative.


## 7 *Jigoku Zōshi*
(The Scroll of Hells)

Attributed to Mitsunaga.
Early Kamakura period (12th century).
Color on paper.
Two scrolls.
Height 26.06 and 22.66 cm.
One scroll in the Nara National Museum.
One scroll in the National Museum, Tokyo.
National Treasure.


These scrolls depict the various hells described in the Buddhist sutras. In the scroll owned by the Nara National Museum, seven hells are portrayed, while there are four hells in the National Museum scroll. The former scroll pictures the sufferings in hell of people who, in their former existence, have committed robbery, killed living creatures, failed to follow the Buddhist law, etc. In the National Museum scroll, the sufferings in hell of those who have sold watered wine or taken advantage of people under the influence of alcohol are depicted. The line and coloring in both scrolls are superlative. The work is doubtfully attributed to Mitsunaga, an eminent artist of the late 12th century.

## 8 *Gaki Zōshi*
### (The Scroll of Hungry Ghosts)

Attributed to Mitsunaga.
Early Kamakura period (12th century).
Color on paper.
Height 26.26 cm.
One scroll in the National Museum, Tokyo.
One scroll in the Kyoto National Museum.
National Treasure.

      Ugly and deformed starving spirits are the subject of these scrolls. The scroll at the National Museum shows ghosts consuming human excrement and cadavers, and being tortured mercilessly by devils and eagles. The scroll owned by the Kyoto National Museum depicts ghosts suffering from hunger and thirst, and being saved by Buddha. Both scrolls are based on accounts of "hungry ghosts" in the Buddhist sutras and make excellent use of line and thin coloring. The work is attributed to Mitsunaga, an eminent artist of the 12th century, but this is not definite.

## 9 *Yamai no Sōshi*
## (The Scroll of Diseases and Deformities)

Attributed to Mitsunaga.
Early Kamakura period (12th century).
Color on paper.
Height 26.06 cm.
In the collection of Sekido Arihiko, Aichi.
National Treasure.

This scroll depicts various human diseases and deformities. Originally there was a series of fifteen pictures on one scroll, but only nine remain today. These show a man afflicted by palsy, a man with an additional small tongue, twin boys, a man with an eye disease, a man with loose teeth, a man with more than one anus, a man with lice, a woman with epilepsy, and a woman with bad breath. Each picture has now been cut and mounted. The paintings employ a free line; they are extremely photographic, yet avoid coarseness, and the scroll can be accounted a masterpiece of the *yamato-e*. The work is attributed to Mitsunaga, a famous painter of the late Heian period (12th century).

## 10 *Kokawa-dera Engi*
## (The Legends of Kokawa-dera Temple)

Artist unknown.
Early Kamakura period (13th century).
Color on paper.
One scroll.
Height 30.6 cm.
Owned by Kokawa-dera, Wakayama.
National Treasure.

This scroll depicts two stories concerning the Senju Kannon of Kokawa Temple in Wakayama Prefecture. The first story is about a young child who begs a night's lodging from a hunter, and makes a Senju (Thousand-armed) Kannon to express his gratitude. The second story shows the Senju Kannon taking the form of a young child in the house of the lord of Kōchi and healing his seriously ill daughter. The scroll is executed in pale coloring and lines of excellent simplicity and sweep.

## 11 Kegon Engi
### (The History of Kegon)

Artist unknown.
Kamakura period (13th century)
Six scrolls.
Height 31.51 cm.
Owned by Kōzan-ji, Kyoto.
National Treasure.

This scroll presents the biographies of two high Buddhist prelates, Gengyō and Gishō, who were the founders of the Kegon sect in Korea in the 7th century. The story tells how Gengyō and Gishō start off together for T'ang China in pursuit of the truth, but on the way Gengyō reaches a kind of enlightenment and returns to Japan to become a prelate famous for his high wisdom and virtue. Gishō reaches China and pursues his studies, but a beautiful woman called Zemmyō falls in love with him in Chang'an. Zemmyō follows Gishō when he finishes his studies and starts back to Japan, throwing herself into the sea and changing into a dragon which protects his ship. The scroll, done in pale colors and superb lines, exhibits a particular skill in its expression of action. Some are of the opinion that it was painted by Seinin, an artist-priest of the Takayama-dera Temple.


## 12 *Kibi Daijin Nittō Ekotoba*
## (The Story of the Minister Kibi's Trip to China)

Attributed to Mitsunaga.
Kamakura period (13th century).
Color on paper.
One scroll.
Height 32.12 cm.
In the Boston Museum.


This story depicts the famous scholar Kibi no Makibi (693-775), an Imperial court retainer, in T'ang China as an ambassador. While he is in China, the T'ang Imperial court presents many difficult problems to test his ability. Makibi is aided by the spirit of Abe no Nakamaro who takes the form of a ghost. (Abe no Nakamaro was a literary scholar of the Nara period who went to study in China and was given an important post by Emperor Hsüang Sung of China. He lived there more than fifty years and died there.)

Together with the use of thick pigments, the work uses a strongly individual, almost exaggerated, line. A marked characteristic in the composition is the repeated appearance of the same character against the same background. The length of the entire scroll is 2,441.72 centimeters, which makes it one of the longest scrolls existing.

## 13 Taima Mandara Engi
## (The Legends of the Taima Mandara)

Artist unknown.
Kamakura period (13th century).
Color on paper.
Two scrolls.
Height 47.79 cm.
Owned by Kōmyō-ji, Kanagawa.
National Treasure.

This scroll depicts the legend concerning the mandara preserved in the Taima Temple in Nara Prefecture. In the Nara period (8th century), an incarnation of Amitabha appears in answer to the supplication of the daughter of Minister Yokohaki and weaves a picture of paradise from a lotus thread. The daughter, in her last moments, is welcomed by Amitabha into paradise.

This scroll, as a picture scroll, achieves a rarely seen adroitness of composition in the large scenes. The subtle and fine line is highly polished, and the use of soft and refined colors with much gold gives it a rich appearance, producing a darkly golden-hued work. Among the scrolls, this work has been preserved as an orthodox representative of the *yamato-e*.

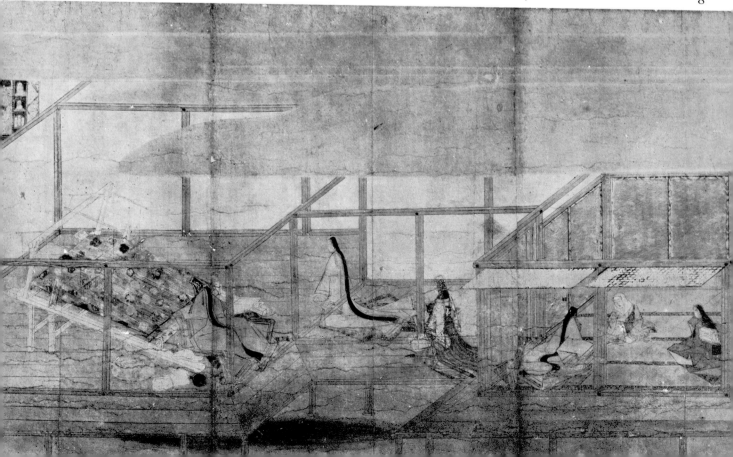

## 14 Kitano Tenjin Engi
### (The Legends of Kitano Tenjin Shrine)

Artist unknown.
Kamakura period (13th century).
Color on paper.
Eight scrolls.
Height 51.52 cm.
Owned by the Kitano Temman-gū, Kyoto.
National Treasure.

This scroll depicts the life of Sugawara Michizane (845-903), an eminent poet and scholar of the Imperial court in the early Heian period, and the historical events subsequent to his death. Following his death, Michizane was deified at Kitano, Kyoto, where he was revered as the deity of scholarship.

This is the oldest and best among the many scrolls concerning Sugawara Michizane. Bright mineral pigments (*iwa-enogu*) are used in this work, and the scenes have a breadth which is rarely seen among picture scrolls. The surface available is unusually wide for a picture scroll; the lines have a noble sweep and the scenes are full of vigor. All in all, there is a sense of massiveness absent from most *yamato-e* scrolls.

## 15 *Sanjūroku Kasen Emaki*
## (The Portraits of Thirty-six Famous Poets)

Attributed to Fujiwara Nobuzane.
Kamakura period (13th century).
Color on paper.
Originally two scrolls.
Height 36.06 cm.
Scattered among various owners.
Important Cultural Property.


This scroll is a series of portraits of thirty-six eminent poets rang-ing from the Nara period through the Heian period (end of the 7th century to the 10th century). To the right of each portrait appear a short biog-raphy and a representative poem. Originally there were two scrolls, but today the individual portraits have been cut and made into separate *kakefuku* (hanging pictures). These portraits, though they depict historical personages, are painted in as fresh and individual manner as if they were sketched from real life. The coloring has a refined brilliance, particular care being lavished on the patterns of the costumes. The work is attributed to Fujiwara Nobu-zane (1176-?), a well-known painter of the Imperial court in the Kama-kura period.

## 16 *Murasaki Shikibu Nikki Emaki*
(Lady Murasaki's Diary)

Attributed to Fujiwara Nobuzane.
Kamakura period (13th century).
Color on paper.
Three scrolls and a number of separate pictures.
Height 21.21 cm.
In the Fujita Art Museum, Osaka; the Gotō Art Museum, Tokyo; and elsewhere.
National Treasure and Important Cultural Property.

This work is based on scenes from ''The Diary of Murasaki Shikibu'' (early 11th century), written by the celebrated authoress of ''The Tales of Genji'' in mid-Heian times. She was a lady-in-waiting to Akiko, the wife of Emperor Ichijō, and all the scenes concern the life of the nobility in the Imperial court. Only a few scrolls exist today, but originally there were probably many more. Thick pigments, silver, and dark gold are used in the paintings to produce an effect of richness. As a portrayal of the

life and manners of the Heian period nobility it is an important reference source, along with the *Genji* scroll.  The work is attributed to Fujiwara Nobuzane (13th century), an eminent artist of the Kamakura period, but this is open to question.

## 17  Heiji Monogatari Emaki
### (The Stories of the Heiji Civil War)

Artist unknown.
Kamakura period (13th century).
Color on paper.
One scroll.
Height 42.42 cm.
In the National Museum, Tokyo.
National Treasure.

The subject matter of this scroll is the Heiji wars, the civil conflicts brought about by rival groups of nobility in 1159, at the end of the Heian period.  This is part of a series, with one scroll in the Boston Museum and one scroll in the Seika-dō.  The scroll in the National Museum, Tokyo is the last of the three.  This scroll pictures the events from the imprisonment of Emperor Nijō by the rebel troops of Fujiwara Nobuyori and Minamoto no Yoshitomo, his escape from the palace to the Rokuhara mansion of Taira no Kiyomori, and the chagrin of Nobuyori when he learns of the escape.

The work exhibits an extremely clever composition in group scenes, a delicate line, and rich, thick pigments.  The refinement of its technique

92 *Heiji Monogatari Emaki*

makes it one of the best picture scrolls of the Kamakura period. The scrolls in the Boston Museum and the National Museum in Tokyo were painted by the same artist. The scenes portraying the burning of the Sanjōdono of the Goshirakawa Palace by Fujiwara Nobuyori and the movements of soldiers are particularly fine. Excellent reference material on the clothing of Japanese warriors is contained in these scrolls.

## 18 *Zuishin Teiki Emaki* (The Imperial Guard Cavalry)

Artist unknown.
Kamakura period (13th century).
Color washes on paper.
One scroll.
Height 26.79 cm.
Owned by Ōkura Kishichirō, Tokyo.
National Treasure.

93 *Zuishin Teiki Emaki*

Nine members of the Imperial Guard and eight cavalry horses of the Heian period (12th century) and the Kamakura period (13th century) are pictured in this scroll. For the most part, it is rendered in *sumi* (black ink) line, and only a small amount of thin coloring is applied to the faces and to the trappings of the horses. The facial expressions of the humans and the attitudes of the horses are full of vitality and individuality. This work is one of the best of the ink line portraits of the Kamakura period. It is attributed to the famous Imperial court painter of the 13th century, Fujiwara Nobuzane.

## *19  Saigyō Monogatari Emaki*
## (The Biography of Priest Saigyō)

Artist  unknown.
Kamakura  period  (13th  century).
Color  on  paper.
Two  scrolls.
Height  31.81  cm.
One  scroll  in  the  Reimei-kai,  Tokyo.
One  scroll  in  the  collection  of  Ōhara  Sōichirō,  Okayama.
Important  Cultural  Property.

This  scroll  depicts  episodes  from  the  life  of  Saigyō  (1118-1190),
a  priest-poet  of  the  late  Heian  and  early  Kamakura  Periods.   Saigyō,  whose
ordinary  name  was  Satō  Norikiyo,  served  as  a  warrior  under  Emperor
Toba,  but  he  perceived  the  transitoriness  of  life  at  the  age  of  twenty-
three  and  became  a  priest.   He  wandered  from  province  to  province  and
became  famous  as  a  nature  poet.   Originally  there  were  probably  a  large
number  of  scrolls,  but  only  two  scrolls  remain  today.   The  scroll  in  the

Reimei-kai portrays the period from Saigyō's decision to become a priest to the time when he takes his vows.   The Ōhara scroll depicts his wanderings in Yoshino and Kumano as the priest Saigyō.   This work has light coloring, delicate lines, and an overall atmosphere of tranquillity.   It is a specimen of the *yamato-e*.

## 20   *Mōko Shūrai Ekotoba*
### (Stories of the Mongolian Invasion)

Attributed to Tosa no Nagataka and Nagaaki.
Kamakura period (13th century).
Color on paper.
Two scrolls.
Height 39.39 cm.
Imperial Household Collection.

These scrolls are also called *Takezaki Suenaga Ekotoba*.   They are chiefly concerned with the exploits of the hero Takezaki Suenaga during the attempted invasion of Japan by the Mongols of Kublai Khan. Suenaga, a warrior of Higo province (Kumamoto Prefecture), fought bravely against the invaders in the two campaigns, in the eleventh year of Bun-ei (1274) and in the fourth year of Kōan, in the Hakata area of Kyūshū. Accordingly, there is no reference to the general progress of the battles during the Mongolian invasion, but a detailed picture of the actual battle conditions in local areas during that period is presented. Thick pigments and a comparatively heavy line are used in the painting. The detailed depiction of armor and helmets, clothing, etc. makes it a good source of information on the accoutrements of war.

## 21 Tōsei Eden
### (The Journey East)

By Rengyō.
Kamakura period (1298).
Color on paper.
Five scrolls.
Height 37.27 cm.
In the Tōshōdai-ji, Nara.
Important Cultural Property.

This scroll depicts the journey from China to Japan of Ganjin (688-763), the Chinese priest who founded the Tōshōdai-ji Temple in Nara, and his spreading of the teachings of the Ritsu sect. Ganjin is portrayed

from the time he took the tonsure at the Tayün Temple in Yang Province at the age of fourteen until his death at the Tōshōdai-ji Temple. Included are his plans to come to Japan at the request of Eiei and Fushō, Japanese priests who were studying in China, and the many perils he underwent before he arrived in Japan. Since this story has mainly China for a background, the style differs from that of other picture scrolls, showing the influence of the Sung period.

## 22 *Ippen Shōnin Eden*
## (The Biography of Saint Ippen)

By En-i.
Kamakura period (1299).
Color on silk.
Twelve scrolls.
Height 38.18 cm.
In the Kankikō-ji, Kyoto, and the National Museum, Tokyo.
National Treasure.

97   *Ippen Shōnin Eden*

This scroll depicts the life of Saint Ippen (1239-89), the founder of the Ji sect.   Ippen established the Ji sect at the time a new Buddhistic fervor was rising in the Kamakura period.   He was a great priest who worked for the popularization of Amidism, and spent most of his life traveling around Japan preaching the *Nembutsu* (a prayer to Amitabha) to all classes.   There are many scrolls which portray the biography of Ippen, but this work is the best.   A disciple of Ippen, Seikai, wrote his biography, and En-i painted it.   It was finished in 1299, only ten years after the death of Ippen.   This work is of great interest as a vivid record of the society and manners of the period during which Ippen lived. A great deal of landscape is portrayed in these scrolls, and nature is presented poetically and with superb technique.   In the depiction of land-scape, these scrolls are unrivaled.   Of the twelve scrolls, only the seventh is in the National Museum.

## 23 *Ishiyama-dera Engi*
(The Legends of Ishiyama-dera Temple)

Attributed to Takashina Takakane, Tosa Mitsunobu, Awataguchi Takamitsu.
Kamakura period, Muromachi period, Edo period (14th, 15th, 16th centuries).
Color on paper.
Seven scrolls.
Height 33.64 cm.
Owned by Ishiyama-dera, Shiga Prefecture.
Important Cultural Property.

This scroll covers the period from the establishment of Ishiyama-dera Temple in Shiga Prefecture by the great priest Rōben, with Nyoirin Kannon as the principal image, to the donation of an estate to the temple by Emperor Godaigo when he ascended the throne in 1318. The history of the temple and the many miracles attributed to the principal deity are combined. The first, second, and third scrolls are attributed to Takashina

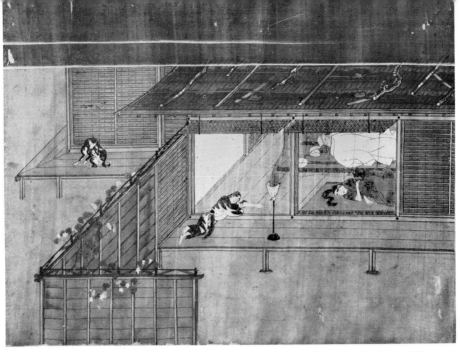

99  *Kasuga Gongen Reigen Ki*

Takakane (14th century), the fourth to Tosa Mitsunobu (15th century), and the fifth to Awataguchi Takamitsu (15th century). The sixth and seventh scrolls were replaced and supplemented by Tani Bunchō (19th century) in the Edo (Tokugawa) period. Of these scrolls, the first, second, and third are the best, with beautiful coloring and soft, fluid lines. It is a work showing the typical characteristics of *yamato-e* painting.

## 24  *Kasuga Gongen Reigen Ki*
## (The Legends of the Kasuga Gongen Miracles)

By Takashina Takakane.
Kamakura period (1309).
Color on silk.
Two scrolls.
Height 41.21 cm.
In the Imperial Household Collection.

These scrolls were originally owned by the Kasuga Shrine in Nara, but they were later presented to the Imperial Household. They were first donated to the Kasuga Shrine by the Minister of the Right, Saionji Kinhira, in March of the second year of Enkei (1309). The work shows the many miracles and wonders connected with the Kasuga deity, the tutelary deity of the Fujiwara family. The painting is executed with great reverence and care for detail. The colors are remarkably rich, with an almost startling brilliance at times. The work has great significance as one of the best achievements of the *yamato-e* picture scroll in the late Kamakura period and as a source of information on the manners of the time.

## 25 *Hōnen Shōnin Eden*
## (The Biography of Saint Hōnen)

Attributed to Yoshimitsu, Kunitaka, Nagataka, Nagaaki, Korehisa, Yuki-mitsu, Mitsuaki, Tamenobu.
Kamakura period (11th century).
Color on paper.
Forty-eight scrolls.
Height 32.73 cm.
In the Chion-in, Kyoto.
National Treasure.

These scrolls portray the life of Hōnen (1133-1212), the founder of the Jōdo (Pure Land) sect, and a large number of Hōnen's important sermons are included in the text. There are many scrolls depicting the

life of Hōnen, but according to tradition these scrolls were specially ordered by Emperor Gofushimi. They are the largest in number and the most successful. The work is attributed to the combined efforts of eight artists, but as there is a great disparity in their periods room for further study remains. Diverse styles are apparent and an overall unity is lacking, but for the most part the scrolls are painted with scrupulous care and beautiful coloring. This work, the most voluminous among existing picture scrolls, includes all classes of people, from the Emperor and the Imperial family down to common people, prostitutes, and beggars. They are of great value in studying the manners of the time.

## 26 *Eshi no Sōshi*
## (The Story of a Painter)

Artist unknown.
Kamakura period (14th century).
Color on paper.
One scroll.
Height 30 cm.
In the Imperial Household Collection.

This scroll tells the story of a destitute painter. A certain down-and-out painter is appointed to be an official in the province of Iyo (Shikoku) and holds a feast in celebration, but his joy is short-lived. The lands of his fief have been taken over by another, and he will receive no land dues. He appeals to a nobleman in charge of painting at the court, but nothing comes of it. Falling still further into poverty, he eventually places his son in a temple and himself resolves to follow the way of Buddha. Both pathos and humor are portrayed in this story.

The painting employs a thick, heavy line, and the faces and figures of the people are represented with great exaggeration. The work has a strong vein of coarse humor and lacks any atmosphere of elegance, but it possesses a certain realistic strength.


## 27 Komakurabe Gyōkō Emaki
## (The Story of an Imperial Visit to the Horse Race)

Artist unknown.
Kamakura period (14th century).
Color on paper.
Two scrolls.
Height 31.52 to 33.93 cm.
One scroll in the Seika-dō, Tokyo.
One scroll in the possession of Sanjō Saneharu, Tokyo.
Important Cultural Property.

These scrolls illustrate the "Koma-kurabe" (horse-racing) scene from the "Tales of Splendor" (11th century), historical stories dealing chiefly with the splendor of the Fujiwara nobility which flourished in the Heian period. They portray scenes from the visit of the Empress Dowager Akiko and the Emperor Goichijō to the Fujiwara mansion in the first year of Manju (1024), and give a good idea of one side of the life and manners of the nobility during the Heian period. The coloring is rich, and the painting is bright and beautiful.

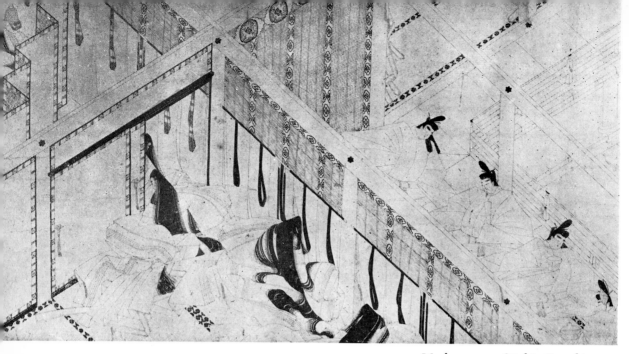

*Makura no Sōshi Emaki*

## 28  *Makura no Sōshi Emaki*
(The Pillow Book)

Artist unknown.
Kamakura period (14th century).
Ink on paper (*boku-ga*).
One scroll.
Height 25.45 cm.
In the possession of Asano Nagatake, Tokyo.
Important Cultural Property.

Seven scenes of life in the Imperial court are selected for illustration
from "The Pillow Book" (10th century) of Sei Shōnagon.  (Sei Shōnagon,
a talented woman familiar with both Japanese and Chinese learning, served
as lady-in-waiting to the Empress Sadako, the wife of Emperor Ichijō.) The
lines of this scroll are in ink, the hair, the eyebrows, and the interior
fittings executed in thicker ink.  A little red is added for the lips.  The
line is extremely delicate and sensitive and the work is a model for
the *yamato-e* in Chinese ink.

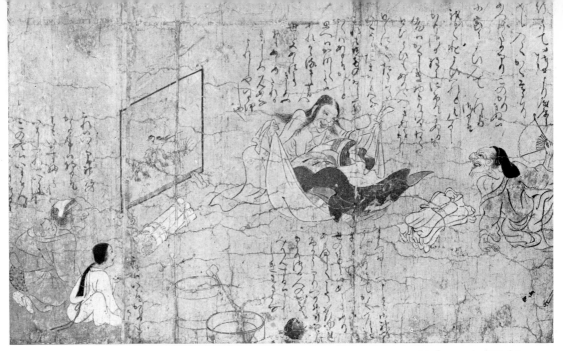

103 *Fukutomi Zōshi*

## 29 *Fukutomi Zōshi*
### (The Story of Fukutomi)

Artist unknown.
Muromachi period (15th century).
Color on paper.
Two scrolls.
Height 31.21 cm.
In the Myōshin-ji, Kyōto.
Important Cultural Property.


These scrolls portray the story of an old man who comes to grief through trying to imitate others. A destitute old man called Hidetake has a dream in which a small bell is given him by a deity. The scroll then relates how Hidetake masters the art of farting and becomes rich as a favorite of the nobility. Fukutomi, another poor old man who lives next door to Hidetake, feels envious, but has a terrible experience when he fails in an attempt to imitate him.

The faces and movements of the characters are rendered realistically,

and their emotions are vividly expressed. Dialogue is included in the pictures themselves in an attempt to make the development of the story smoother. This is one of the best of the picture scrolls illustrating popular tales of the Muromachi period.

## 30　*Dōjō-ji Engi*
### (The Legends of Dōjō-ji Temple)

Artist unknown.
Muromachi period. (16th century).
Color on paper.
Two scrolls.
Height 31.52 cm.
In the Dōjō-ji, Wakayama Prefecture.
Important Cultural Property.

During the reign of Emperor Daigo (10th century), a young priest from Ōshū who goes to worship at Kumano in the province of Kii

(Wakayama Prefecture) is loved by another man's wife. When the priest refuses her love and flees, the woman pursues him and turns into a big snake. The priest hides in the bell of the Dōjō-ji Temple and is burned to death by the fiery breath from the snake's mouth. However, in answer to the prayers of the priests of the Dōjō-ji Temple, the woman and the priest are brought together as heavenly beings. The work is of poor quality and awkward technique, and shows typical characteristics of the popular picture scrolls of the Muromachi period.

# List of *Emaki* and Their English Titles

Notes :

( 1 )   Almost all surviving picture scrolls of any artistic value are included in this list.

( 2 )   The marks ○, ◎, and ⊙ indicate items registered by the Japanese Government as National Treasures, Important Cultural Properties, and Important Art Objects respectively.

( 3 )   Abbreviations :

Attrib. = Attributed

Coll.   = Collection

| TITLE | No. of scrolls |
|---|---|
| *Aki no Yo no Nagamonogatari Emaki*<br>(Tales of an Autumn Night) | 3 |
| ○ *Ashibiki Emaki*<br>(Story of a Priest and His Minion) | 5 |
| ◎ *Bai Sōshi*<br>(Scroll of Veterinary Gods and Herbs) | 1 |
| ◎ *Bai Sōshi* | 1 segment |
| ◎ *Bai Sōshi* | 1 segment |
| *Bakemono Zōshi*<br>(Tales of Spirits) | 1 |
| ◉ *Ban Dainagon Ekotoba*<br>(Story of the Courtier Ban Dainagon) | 3 |
| ◎ *Boki Ekotoba*<br>(Biography of Priest Kakunyo) | 10 |
| ◎ *Bukki-gun Emaki*<br>(Story of Buddhas and Goblins) | 1 |
| ◎ *Chigo Kannon Engi*<br>(Legend of the Chigo Kannon) | 1 |
| *Chigo Zōshi*<br>(Secret Scenes of a Priest and His Minion) | 1 |
| ◉ *Chōjū Jimbutsu Giga*<br>(Cartoons of Animals and Humans) | 4 |
| ◎ *Chūden Gyokai Zukan*<br>(Portraits of Emperor and Courtiers Gathered in the Central Hall of the Imperial Palace) | 1 |

| ARTIST | OWNER | Period & century (A.D.) |
|---|---|---|
| | Anonymous coll. | Muromachi, 16th |
| | Itsuō Art Museum, Osaka | Muromachi, 16th |
| | Tokyo National Museum | Kamakura, 13th |
| | Mrs. Kawasugi Hatsu | Kamakura, 13th |
| | Mr. Kosaka Junzō | Kamakura, 13th |
| | Mr. Minakami Zen-ichirō | Muromachi, 16th |
| Attrib. to Tokiwa Mitsu-naga | Mr. Sakai Tadahiro | Heian, 12th |
| Fujiwara Takaaki, Taka-masa & Hisanobu | Nishi Hongan-ji, Kyoto | Kamakura, 14th |
| | Jūnen-ji, Kyoto | Muromachi, 15th |
| | Mr. Murayama Nagataka | Kamakura, 14th |
| | Sambō-ji, Kyoto | Kamakura, 14th |
| Attrib. to Kakuyū | Kōzan-ji, Kyoto | Scrolls 1 & 2, Heian, 12th; 3 & 4, Kamakura, 13th |
| Copied from original by Fujiwara Nobuzane | Mr. Kujō Michihide | Muromachi, 14th |

| TITLE | No. of scrolls |
|---|---|
| *Daibutsu-den Engi*<br>(Legends of Daibutsu-den Hall in Tōdai-ji Temple) | 3 |
| ◎ *Dōjō-ji Engi*<br>(Legends of Dōjō-ji Temple) | 2 |
| ○ *Dōjō-ji Engi* | 1 |
| ◎ *Egara Tenjin Engi*<br>(Legends of Egara Tenjin Shrine) | 3 |
| ◉ *E Inga-kyō*<br>(Sutra of Cause and Effect) | 1 |
| ◉ *E Inga-kyō* | 1 |
| ◉ *E Inga-kyō* | 1 |
| ◎ *E Inga-kyō* | 1 |
| *E Inga-kyō* | 1 |
| ◎ *E Inga-kyō* | 1 |
| ◎ *E Inga-kyō* | 1 |
| *Eshi no Sōshi*<br>(Story of a Painter) | 1 |
| ◎ *Fudō Riyaku Engi*<br>(Legend of Fudō's Blessing) | 1 |

| ARTIST | OWNER | Period & century (A.D.) |
|---|---|---|
| Shiba Rinken | Tōdai-ji, Nara | Muromachi, 16th |
| | Dōjō-ji, Wakayama | Muromachi, 16th |
| | Mr. Sakai Tadamasa | Muromachi, 16th |
| Fujiwara Yukinaga | Maeda Ikutoku-kai Foundation, Tokyo | Kamakura, 14th |
| | Jōbonrendai-ji, Kyoto | Nara, 8th |
| | Hōon-in, Kyoto | Nara, 8th |
| | Tokyo University of Arts | Nara, 8th |
| | Atami Art Museum, Shizuoka (formerly in Masuda Coll.) | Nara, 8th |
| | Prince Kuni | Nara, 8th |
| Keinin & Shōjumaru | Nezu Art Museum, Tokyo | Kamakura, 13th |
| Keinin & Shōjumaru | Gotō Art Museum, Tokyo (formerly in Daitōkyū Memorial Library) | Kamakura, 13th |
| | Imperial Coll. | Kamakura, 14th |
| | Tokyo National Museum | Kamakura, 14th |

| TITLE | No. of scrolls |
|---|---|
| ◎ *Fujinamie Zōshi*<br>(Poem-story of a Courtier's Love) | 1 |
| ◎ *Fukutomi Zōshi*<br>(Story of Fukutomi) | 2 |
| ◉ *Gaki Zōshi*<br>(Scroll of Hungry Ghosts) | 1 |
| ◉ *Gaki Zōshi* | 1 |
| ◉ *Genji Monogatari Emaki*<br>(Tales of Genji) | 43 segments<br>(originally 3<br>scrolls) |
| ◉ *Genji Monogatari Emaki* | 13 segments<br>(originally 1<br>scroll) |
| ◎ *Go-sannen Kassen Emaki*<br>(Stories of the Go-sannen Civil War) | 3 |
| ◎ *Hakone Gongen Engi*<br>(Legend of Hakone Gongen Shrine) | 1 |
| *Hase-dera Engi*<br>(Legends of Hase-dera Temple) | 6 |
| ◎ *Haseo-kyō Zōshi*<br>(Story of Lord Haseo) | 1 |
| ◉ *Heiji Monogatari Emaki*<br>(Stories of the Heiji Civil War)<br>—Scroll on "The Imperial Visit to Rokuhara"— | 1 |
| ◎ *Heiji Monogatari Emaki*<br>—Scroll on "Shinzei"— | 1 |

| ARTIST | OWNER | Period & century (A.D.) |
|---|---|---|
|  | Mr. Asada Chōhei | Kamakura, 14th |
|  | Shumpo-in in Myōshin-ji, Kyoto | Muromachi, 15th |
| Attrib. to Tokiwa Mitsunaga | Kyoto National Museum (formerly in Sōgen-ji) | Kamakura, 12th |
| Attrib. to Tokiwa Mitsunaga | Tokyo National Museum (formerly in Kawamoto Coll.) | Kamakura, 12th |
| Attrib. to Fujiwara Takayoshi | Tokugawa Reimei-kai Foundation, Tokyo | Heian, 12th |
| Attrib. to Fujiwara Takayoshi | Gotō Art Museum, Tokyo (formerly in Masuda Coll.) | Heian, 12th |
| Hidanokami Korehisa | Tokyo National Museum (formerly in Ikeda Coll.) | Kamakura, 14th |
|  | Hakone Jinja, Kanagawa | Kamakura, 14th |
| Attrib. to Tosa Mitsumochi | Hase-dera, Nara | Muromachi, 16th |
|  | Mr. Hosokawa Moritatsu | Kamakura, 14th |
| Attrib. to Sumiyoshi Keion | Tokyo National Museum | Kamakura, 13th |
|  | Seika-dō Foundation, Tokyo | Kamakura, 14th |

| TITLE | No. of scrolls |
|---|---|
| *Heiji Monogatari Emaki*<br>—Scroll on "Setting Fire to the Sanjō-den"— | 1 |
| *Heike Kindachi Sōshi*<br>(Anecdotes of Noblemen of the Heike Family) | 1 |
| ⊙ *Hōnen Shōnin Eden*<br>(Biography of Saint Hōnen) | 48 |
| ◎ *Hōnen Shōnin Eden* | 48 |
| ◎ *Hōnen Shōnin Eden* | 2 |
| ◎ *Hōnen Shōnin Eden* | 1 |
| ◎ *Hōnen Shōnin Eden*<br>("Kōgan Version") | 1 |
| ◎ *Hōnen Shōnin Eden*<br>("Kōgan Version") | 3 |
| ◎ *Hōnen Shōnin Eden*<br>("Rin-a Version") | 1 |
| ◎ *Hossō-shu Hiji Ekotoba*<br>(Story of Genjō Sanzō, Founder of Hossō Buddhism) | 12 |
| ◎ *Hōyake Amida Engi*<br>(Legend of the Hōyake Buddha) | 2 |
| ◎ *Hyakki Yakō Emaki*<br>(Goblins and Spirits Infesting the Night) | 1 |
| ◎ *Inaba-dō Engi*<br>(Legends of Inaba-dō Temple) | 1 |

| ARTIST | OWNER | Period & century (A.D.) |
|---|---|---|
| Attrib. to Sumiyoshi Keion | Museum of Fine Arts, Boston | Kamakura, 13th |
| | Matsunaga Memorial Museum, Kanagawa | Kamakura, 14th |
| Attrib. to Tosa Yoshi-mitsu & 7 other artists | Chion-in, Kyoto | Kamakura, 14th |
| Attrib. to Tosa Yoshimitsu | Oku-no-in of Taima-dera, Nara | Kamakura, 14th |
| | Zōjō-ji, Tokyo | Kamakura, 14th |
| | Tokyo National Museum | Kamakura, 14th |
| | Chion-in, Kyoto | Kamakura, 14th |
| | Mr. Dōmoto Shirō | Kamakura, 14th |
| | Mr. Tamura Hikoshichi | Kamakura, 14th |
| Attrib. to Takashina Takakane | Fujita Art Museum, Osaka | Kamakura, 14th |
| | Kōsoku-ji, Kanagawa | Kamakura, 14th |
| Attrib. to Tosa Mitsunobu | Shinju-an in Daitoku-ji, Kyoto | Muromachi, 16th |
| | Tokyo National Museum | Kamakura, 14th |

| TITLE | No. of scrolls |
|---|---|
| ○ *In no Dainagon Ekotoba*<br>   (Story of the Courtier In no Dainagon) | 2 |
| ◎ *Ippen Shōnin Eden*<br>   (Biography of Saint Ippen) | 7 |
| ⊙ *Ippen Shōnin Eden*<br>   (Biography of Saint Ippen) | 11 |
| ⊙ *Ippen Shōnin Eden* | 1 |
| ◎ *Ippen Shōnin Eden* | 1 |
| ◎ *Ippen Shōnin Eden* | 10 |
| ◎ *Ippen Shōnin Eden* | 4 |
| ◎ *Ise Monogatari Emaki*<br>   (The Tales of Ise) | 1 |
| ◎ *Ise Shin-Meisho Uta-awase Emaki*<br>   (Poetry Contest on Newly Selected Famous Scenic Spots in Ise Province) | 1 |
| ◎ *Ishiyama-dera Engi*<br>   (Legends of Ishiyama-dera Temple) | 7 |
| *Jidai Fudō Uta-awase*<br>   (Portraits of Poets of Different Periods and Their Poems) | 1<br>(album) |
| ⊙ *Jigoku Zōshi*<br>   (Scroll of Hells) | 1 |

| ARTIST | OWNER | Period & century (A.D.) |
| --- | --- | --- |
| | Matsunaga Memorial Museum, Kanagawa | Kamakura, 14th |
| | Maeda Ikutoku-kai Foundation, Tokyo | Muromachi, 15th |
| En-i | Kankikō-ji, Kyoto | Kamakura, 13th |
| En-i | Tokyo National Museum | Kamakura, 13th |
| | Kindai-ji, Nagano | Kamakura, 14th |
| | Shinkō-ji, Hyogo | Muromachi, 15th |
| | Miei-dō Shin Zenkō-ji, Kyoto | Muromachi, 15th |
| | Mr. Hara Ryōzaburō | Kamakura, 14th |
| Attrib. to Fujiwara Takasuke | Jingūshi-chō, Mie | Kamakura, 13th |
| 5 attrib. to Takakane, Takamitsu & Mitsunobu; 2 by Tani Bunchō | Ishiyama-dera, Shiga | Kamakura, 14th (4th & 5th scrolls, Muromachi; 6th & 7th, Edo) |
| | Tokyo National Museum | Kamakura, 14th |
| Attrib. to Tokiwa Mitsunaga | Nara National Museum (formerly in Hara Coll.) | Kamakura, 12th |

| TITLE | No. of scrolls |
|---|---|
| ◉ *Jigoku Zōshi* | 1 |
| *Jigoku Zōshi* | 1 |
| ◎ *Jingū Kōgō Engi*<br>(Deeds of the Empress Jingū) | 2 |
| *Jizō Engi*<br>(Legends of Jizō) | 1 |
| ◎ *Jōdo Goso Eden*<br>(Biographies of Five Jōdo Patriarchs) | 1 |
| ○ *Jūni-rui Emaki*<br>(Story of the Animals of the Twelve Horary Signs) | 3 |
| ◎ *Jūni Innen Emaki*<br>(Scroll of the Twelve Fates) | 1 |
| ◎ *Kankiten Reigen Ki*<br>(Legends of the Buddhist Divinity Kankiten) | 2 |
| *Kasuga Gongen Reigen Ki*<br>(The Kasuga Gongen Miracles) | 20 |
| ◉ *Kegon Engi*<br>(History of Kegon Buddhism) | 6 |
| ◎ *Kegon Gojūgo-sho Emaki*<br>(Zenzai Dōji's Pilgrimage to the Fifty-five Saints) | 1 |
| ◎ *Kegon Gojūgo-sho Emaki* | 1 |
| ◎ *Kegon Gojūgo-sho Emaki* | 1 |

| ARTIST | OWNER | Period & century (A.D.) |
|---|---|---|
| Attrib. to Tokiwa Mitsunaga | Tokyo National Museum (formerly in Anjū-in) | Kamakura, 12th |
| | Mr. Masuda Yoshinobu | Kamakura, 13th |
| | Konda Hachiman-gū, Osaka | Muromachi, 15th |
| Attrib. to Kose Ariie | Tokyo National Museum | Kamakura, 14th |
| | Kōmyō-ji, Kanagawa | Kamakura, 14th |
| Attrib. to Tosa Mitsuhiro | Mr. Dōmoto Inshō | Muromachi, 15th |
| | Nezu Art Museum, Tokyo | Kamakura, 13th |
| | Mr. Mutō Kinta | Kamakura, 14th |
| Takashina Takakane | Imperial Coll. | Kamakura, 14th |
| | Kōzan-ji, Kyoto | Kamakura, 13th |
| | Tōdai-ji, Nara | Kamakura, 13th |
| | Fujita Art Museum, Osaka | Kamakura, 13th |
| | Mr. Ueno Seiichi | Kamakura, 13th |

| TITLE | No. of scrolls |
|---|---|
| ◎ *Kegon Gojūgo-sho Emaki* | 1 |
| ◎ *Kegon Gojūgo-sho Emaki* | 2 segments |
| ◎ *Kegon Gojūgo-sho Emaki* | 1 |
| ◎ *Kitano Tenjin Engi* (Legends of Kitano Tenjin Shrine) | 3 |
| ⊙ *Kitano Tenjin Engi* (Shōkyū Version) | 9 |
| ◎ *Kitano Tenjin Engi* (Kōan Version) | 2 |
| ◎ *Kitano Tenjin Engi* (Kōan Version) | 2 |
| *Kibi Daijin Nittō Ekotoba* (Story of Minister Kibi's Trip to China) | 1 |
| ◎ *Kiyomizu-dera Engi* (Legends of Kiyomizu-dera Temple) | 3 |
| ◎ *Kōbō Daishi Gyōjō Ekotoba* (Biography of Kōbō Daishi) | 12 |
| ⊙ *Kokawa-dera Engi* (Legends of Kokawa-dera Temple) | 1 |
| ◎ *Komakurabe Gyōkō Emaki* (Story of an Imperial Visit to the Horse race) | 1 |
| ◎ *Komakurabe Gyōkō Emaki* | 1 |

| ARTIST | OWNER | Period & century (A.D.) |
| --- | --- | --- |
| | Mr. Tomoda Hiroshi | Kamakura, 13th |
| | Tokyo National Museum | Kamakura, 13th |
| | Mr. Hara Kunizō | Kamakura, 14th |
| Tosa Mitsunobu | Kitano Temman-gū, Kyoto | Muromachi, 15th |
| Attrib. to Fujiwara Nobuzane | Kitano Temman-gū, Kyoto | Kamakura, 13th |
| Attrib. to Tosa Yukimitsu | Kitano Temman-gu, Kyoto | Kamakura, 13th |
| Attrib. to Tosa Yukimitsu | Tokyo National Museum | Kamakura, 13th |
| Attrib. to Tokiwa Mitsunaga | Museum of Fine Arts, Boston (formerly in Sakai Coll.) | Kamakura, 13th |
| Tosa Mitsunobu | Tokyo National Museum | Muromachi, 16th |
| | Kyōōgokoku-ji, Kyoto | Kamakura, 14th |
| Attrib. to Kakuyū | Kokawa-dera, Wakayama | Kamakura, 13th |
| | Mr. Kubo Sōtarō | Kamakura, 14th |
| | Seika-dō Foundation, Tokyo | Kamakura, 14th |

| TITLE | No. of scrolls |
|---|---|
| ◎ *Kōmyō Shingon Kudoku Ekotoba*<br>(The Virtues of the Kōmyō Shingon Spell) | 3 |
| ◎ *Konda Sōbyō Engi*<br>(Legends of Konda Hachiman Shrine) | 3 |
| *Koshibagaki Zōshi*<br>(Romance by the Brushwood Fence) | 1 |
| *Kotohara Emaki*<br>(Poem-story of a Lute) | 1 |
| ◎ *Kōya Daishi Gyōjō Zuga*<br>(Biography of Kōbō Daishi) | 6 |
| ◎ *Kuge Retsuei Zukan*<br>(Scroll of Portraits of Courtiers) | 1 |
| ◎ *Kuwanomi-dera Engi*<br>(Legends of Kuwanomi-dera Temple) | 2 |
| ◎ *Makura no Sōshi Emaki*<br>(The Pillow Book) | 1 |
| ◎ *Matsuzaki Tenjin Engi*<br>(Legends of Matsuzaki Tenjin Shrine) | 6 |
| *Mōko Shūrai Ekotoba*<br>(Stories of the Mongol Invasion) | 2 |
| ◎ *Monogatari Emaki*<br>(An Unidentified Story) | 12<br>segments |
| ◎ *Murasaki Shikibu Nikki Emaki*<br>(Lady Murasaki's Diary) | 1 |
| ◉ *Murasaki Shikibu Nikki Emaki* | 1 |

| ARTIST | OWNER | Period & century (A.D.) |
|---|---|---|
| | Myōō-in, Shiga | Muromachi, 14th |
| | Konda Hachiman-gu, Osaka | Muromachi, 15th |
| | Anonymous Coll. | Kamakura, 13th |
| Emperor Gohanazono | Imperial Coll. | Muromachi, 15th |
| Attrib. to Kose no Ari-yasu | Jizō-in, Wakayama | Kamakura, 14th (1st scroll is replacement made in Edo Period) |
| | Kyoto National Museum | Kamakura, 13th |
| Tosa Mitsumochi | Kuwanomi-dera, Shiga | Muromachi, 16th |
| | Mr. Asano Nagatake | Kamakura, 14th |
| | Bōfu Temman-gū, Yamaguchi | Kamakura, 14th |
| Attrib. to Tosa Nagataka & Nagaaki | Imperial Coll. | Kamakura, 13th |
| | Tokugawa Reimei-kai Funda-tion, Tokyo | Kamakura, 14th |
| | Mr. Hachisuka Masauji | Kamakura, 13th |
| | Fujita Art Museum, Osaka | Kamakura, 13th |

| TITLE | No. of scrolls |
|---|---|
| ⊙ *Murasaki Shikibu Nikki Emaki* | 6 segments |
| ◎ *Murasaki Shikibu Nikki Emaki* | 1 segment |
| ◎ *Murasaki Shikibu Nikki Emaki* | 1 |
| ◎ *Murasaki Shikibu Nikki Emaki* | 1 |
| ◎ *Naki Fudō Engi*<br>(Legend of the Weeping Fudō) | 1 |
| ◎ *Naomoto Mōshibumi Ekotoba*<br>(Story of the Courtier Naomoto) | 1 |
| ◎ *Nayotake Monogatari Emaki*<br>(Tale of the Emperor Gosaga) | 1 |
| *Nenjū Gyōji Emaki*<br>(Annual Functions in the Imperial Court) | 16 |
| ⊙ *Nezame Monogatari Emaki*<br>(The Nezame Monogatari) | 1 |
| *Nichiren Shōnin Chūga-san*<br>(Biography of Saint Nichiren) | 5 |
| *Nigatsu-dō Engi*<br>(Legends of the Nigatsu-dō Hall in Tōdai-ji Temple) | 2 |
| ◎ *Nōe Hōshi Ekotoba*<br>(Legend of Priest Nōe) | 1 |
| ◎ *Obusuma Saburō Ekotoba*<br>(Story of the Warrior Obusuma Saburō) | 1 |

| ARTIST | OWNER | Period & century (A.D.) |
|---|---|---|
| | Gotō Art Museum, Tokyo (formerly in Morikawa Coll.) | Kamakura, 13th |
| | Mrs. Ōkura Kame (formerly in Morikawa Coll.) | Kamakura, 13th |
| | Mr. Morikawa Kaoru | Kamakura, 13th |
| | Mr. Hisamatsu Satakoto | Kamakura, 13th |
| | Shōjōke-in, Kyoto | Muromachi, 15th |
| Attrib. to Tosa Mitsuaki | Mrs. Kamei Michiko | Kamakura, 14th |
| | Kotohira-gū, Kagawa | Kamakura, 14th |
| Copied from original; attrib. to Tokiwa Mitsunaga | Mr. Tanaka Shimbi | Edo, 17th |
| | Museum Yamato Bunka-kan, Nara | Heian, 12th |
| Kubota Tōtai | Honkoku-ji, Kyoto | Muromachi, 16th |
| | Tōdai-ji, Nara | Muromachi, 16th |
| | Kōryū-ji, Kyoto | Kamakura, 13th |
| Attrib. to Fujiwara Takasuke | Mr. Asano Nagatake | Kamakura, 13th |

| TITLE | No. of scrolls |
|---|---|
| ◎ Ōe-yama Ekotoba<br>   (Story of Goblins on Mt. Ōe) | 2 |
| ◎ Ono no Yukimi Gokō Emaki<br>   (Story of the Imperial Visit to Ono for Snow Viewing) | 1 |
| ◎ Rajū Sanzō Eden<br>   (Biography of Rajū Sanzō) | 1 |
| ○ Sagoromo Monogatari Emaki<br>   (Tale of the Courtier Sagoromo) | segments |
| ◎ Saigyō Monogatari Emaki<br>   (Biography of Priest Saigyō) | 1 |
| ◎ Saigyō Monogatari Emaki | 1 |
| ◎ Sairei Zōshi<br>   (Scroll of Festival Scenes) | 1 |
| Sanjūni-ban Shokunin Uta-awase Emaki<br>   (Record of Poetry Contest of Thirty-two Pairs of Poems by Men of Various Professions) | 1 |
| ◎ Sanjūroku Kasen Emaki<br>   (Portraits of Thirty-six Famous Poets) | segments (originally 2 scrolls) |
| ◎ Sanjūroku Kasen Emaki<br>   ("Agedatami Kasen" Version) | segments |
| ◎ Sannō Reigen Ki<br>   (Legends of the Sanno Minacles) | 1 |
| ◎ Sannō Reigen Ki | 2 |
| ◎ Sannō Reigen Ki | 1 |

| ARTIST | OWNER | Period & century (A.D.) |
| --- | --- | --- |
|  | Itsuō Art Museum, Osaka | Kamakura, 14th |
| Attrib. to Fujiwara Tsunetaka | Tokyo University of Arts | Kamakura, 14th |
|  | Mr. Hosomi Ryō | Muromachi, 15th |
|  | Scattered in Tokyo National Museum & other collections | Kamakura, 14th |
| Attrib. to Fujiwara Tsunetaka | Tokugawa Reimei-kai Foundation, Tokyo | Kamakura, 13th |
| Attrib. to Fujiwara Tsunetaka | Mr. Ōhara Sōichirō (formerly in Hachisuka Coll.) | Kamakura, 13th |
|  | Maeda Ikutoku-kai Foundation, Tokyo | Muromachi, 15th |
|  | Mr. Ishii Ryūsuke | Muromachi, 15th |
| Attrib. to Fujiwara Nobuzane | Scattered in different coll. (originally in Satake Family) | Kamakura, 13th |
| Attrib. to Fujiwara Nobuzane | Scattered in different coll. | Kamakura, 13th |
|  | Hie Jinja, Shizuoka | Kamakura, 13th |
| Attrib. to Rokkaku Jakusai | Mr. Kubo Sōtarō | Muromachi, 15th |
| Attrib. to Rokkaku Jakusai | Mr. Egawa Tokusuke | Muromachi, 15th |

| TITLE | No. of scrolls |
|---|---|
| ◎ *Sannō Reigen Ki* | I |
| ◎ *Seikō-ji Engi*<br>(Legends of Seikō-ji Temple) | 2 |
| ◎ *Seiryō-ji Engi*<br>(Legends of Seiryō-ji Temple) | 6 |
| ◎ *Shakkyō Sanjūroku Kasen Emaki*<br>(Thirty-six Buddhist Saints and Their Poems) | I |
| ◉ *Shigi-san Engi*<br>(Legends of Shigi-san Temple) | 3 |
| *Shikkongō-jin Engi*<br>(Legends of the Deity Shikkongō) | 3 |
| ◎ *Shinnyo-dō Engi*<br>(Legends of Shinnyo-dō Temple) | 3 |
| ◎ *Shinran Shōnin Eden*<br>(Biography of Saint Shinran) | 4 |
| ◎ *Shinran Shōnin Eden* | 4 |
| ◎ *Shinran Shōnin Eden*<br>("Kōgan Version") | 4 |
| ◎ *Shōgun-zuka Emaki*<br>(Story of the Construction of the "Shōgun-zuka") | I |
| ◎ *Shōtoku Taishi Eden*<br>(Biography of Prince Shōtoku) | I |
| ◎ *Shūi Kotoku Den*<br>(Biographies of Saints Hōnen and Shinran) | 9 |

| ARTIST | OWNER | Period & century (A.D.) |
| --- | --- | --- |
| Attrib. to Rokkaku Jakusai | Shōgen-ji, Shiga | Muromachi, 15th |
| Attrib. to Tosa Mitsunobu | Tokyo National Museum | Muromachi, 15th |
| Attrib. to Kano Motonobu | Seiryō-ji, Kyoto | Muromachi, 16th |
| | Tokyo National Museum | Kamakura, 14th |
| Attrib. to Kakuyū | Chōgosonshi-ji, Nara | Heian, 12th |
| Attrib. to Tosa Mitsuhiro | Tōdai-ji, Nara | Muromachi, 16th |
| Kamon-no-suke Hisakuni | Shinshōgokuraku-ji, Kyoto | Muromachi, 16th |
| Sōshun & Enjaku | Higashi Hongan-ji, Kyoto | Kamakura, 14th |
| | Shōgan-ji, Chiba | Kamakura, 14th |
| | Higashi Hongan-ji, Kyoto | Kamakura, 14th |
| Attrib. to Kakuyū | Kōzan-ji, Kyoto | Kamakura, 13th |
| | Jōgū-ji, Ibaragi | Kamakura, 14th |
| | Jōfuku-ji, Ibaragi | Kamakura, 14th |

| TITLE | No. of scrolls |
|---|---|
| ◎ *Sumiyoshi Monogatari Emaki*<br>(Tales of Sumiyoshi) | 1 |
| ◎ *Sumiyoshi Monogatari Emaki* | 2 |
| ◎ *Sungyū Ekotoba*<br>(Portraits of Famous Carriage-bulls) | segments |
| ◉ *Taima Mandara Engi*<br>(Legends of the Taima Mandara) | 2 |
| ○ *Taima-dera Engi*<br>(Legends of Taima-dera Temple) | 3 |
| *Tawara Tōda Emaki*<br>(The Adventure of Tawara Tōda) | 3 |
| *Tennō Sekkan Dajin Ei*<br>(Portraits of Emperors, Regents, Advisors to Emperors, and Ministers) | 3 |
| ◎ *Tennō Sekkan Ei Zukan*<br>(Portraits of Emperors, Regents, and Advisors to Emperors) | 1 |
| ◎ *Tengu Zōshi*<br>(Stories of Conceited Priests) | 2 |
| ◎ *Tengu Zōshi* | 1 |
| ◎ *Tengu Zōshi* | 1 |
| ◎ *Tengu Zōshi* | 1 |
| ◎ *Tōhoku-in Shokunin Uta-awase Emaki*<br>(Record of a Poetry Contest at Tōhoku-in among Men of Various Professions) | 1 |

| ARTIST | OWNER | Period & century (A.D.) |
|---|---|---|
| Attrib. to Tosa Nagataka | Tokyo National Museum | Kamakura, 14th |
| | Seika-dō Foundation, Tokyo | Kamakura, 14th |
| | Scattered in Tokyo National Museum & other coll. | Kamakura, 13th |
| Attrib. to Sumiyoshi Keion | Kōmyō-ji, Kanagawa | Kamakura, 13th |
| Tosa Mitsumochi | Taima-dera, Nara | Muromachi, 16th |
| | Konkaikōmyō-ji, Kyoto | Muromachi, 16th |
| Fujiwara Tamenobu & Gōshin | Imperial Coll. | Kamakura, 13th-14th |
| | Tokugawa Reimei-kai Foundation, Tokyo | Kamakura, 13th-14th |
| | Tokyo National Museum | Kamakura, 13th |
| | Mr. Miyamoto (formerly in Maeda Coll.) | Kamakura, 13th |
| | Mr. Nakamura Yōichirō (formerly in Hisamatsu Coll.) | Kamakura, 13th |
| | Nezu Art Museum, Tokyo | Kamakura, 13th |
| | Tokyo National Museum | Kamakura, 14th |

| TITLE | No. of scrolls |
|---|---|
| ◎ *Tōsei Eden*<br>(The Journey East) | 5 |
| ◎ *Toyo-no-akari Esōshi*<br>The Toyo-no-akari Story) | 1 |
| *Tsuchigumo Zōshi*<br>(Story of Monstrous Spiders) | 1 |
| ○ *Tsurugaoka Hōshō-e Shokunin Uta-awase Emaki*<br>(Record of a Poetry Contest among Men of Various Professions<br>at Hōshō-e Ceremony at Tsurugaoka Shrine) | 1 |
| ⊙ *Yamai no Sōshi*<br>(Scroll of Diseases and Deformities) | 10 segments<br>(originally 1<br>scroll) |
| ◎ *Yareko Tontō Ekotoba*<br>(A Fable about Rebirth in Paradise) | 1 |
| ◎ *Yata Jizō Engi*<br>(Legends of Yata Jizō) | 2 |
| ○ *Yūki Kassen Ekotoba*<br>(Stories of the Civil War between the Ashikaga Government<br>and Yūki Family) | 1 |
| ○ *Yūzū Nembutsu Engi* (Wood-block Print Version)<br>(Stories of the Origin of Yūzū Nembutsu Buddhism) | 2 |
| ○ *Yūzū Nembutsu Engi* | 1 |
| ◎ *Yūzū Nembutsu Engi* | 2 |
| ◎ *Yūzū Nembutsu Engi* | 2 |

| ARTIST | OWNER | Period & century (A.D.) |
|---|---|---|
| Rengyō | Tōshōdai-ji, Nara | Kamakura, 13th |
| | Maeda Ikutoku-kai Foundation, Tokyo | Kamakura, 14th |
| | Tokyo National Museum | Kamakura, 14th |
| | Mr. Yabumoto Sōshirō | Muromachi, 16th |
| Attrib. to Tokiwa Mitsunaga | Mr. Sekido Arihiko | Kamakura, 12th |
| | Tokugawa Reimei-kai Foundation, Tokyo | Kamakura, 14th |
| | Yata-dera, Kyoto | Kamakura, 14th |
| | Mr. Hosomi Ryō | Muromachi, 15th |
| | Dainembutsu-ji, Osaka | Kamakura, 14th |
| | Nezu Art Museum, Tokyo | Kamakura, 14th |
| Attrib. to Tosa Yukihide & 5 other artists | Seiryō-ji, Kyoto | Muromachi, 15th |
| Attrib. to Tosa Mitsunobu | Zenrin-ji, Kyoto | Muromachi, 15th |

| TITLE | No. of scrolls |
|---|---|
| *Zegaibō Ekotoba*<br>(Story of a Goblin Named Zegaibō) | 2 |
| ◎ *Zegaibō Ekotoba* | 1 |
| *Zen-kunen Kassen Emaki*<br>(Stories of the Zen-kunen Civil War) | 1 |
| ◎ *Zenkyōbō Ekotoba*<br>(Sermons by the Priest Zenkyōbō) | 1 |
| ◎ *Zenshin Shōnin Eden* ("Rin-a Version")<br>(Biography of Saint Zenshin) | 2 |
| ⊙ *Zuishin Teiki Emaki*<br>(Imperial Guard Cavalry) | 1 |

| ARTIST | OWNER | (Period & century A.D.) |
|---|---|---|
| | Manshu-in, Kyoto | Kamakura, 14th |
| | Mr. Sumitomo Kichizaemon | Muromachi, 15th |
| | Tokyo National Museum | Kamakura, 14th |
| | Mr. Nishiwaki Saizaburō | Kamakura, 14th |
| | Nishi Hongan-ji, Kyoto | Kamakura, 14th |
| Attrib. to Fujiwara Nobuzane | Mr. Ōkura Kishichirō | Kamakura, 13th |

# Index

(with Japanese characters for proper names and titles of *emaki*)